Plant-Based Perfection

Delicious Vegan Recipes for Every Occasion

Dorinda Woodard

Copyright © 2023

All rights reserved. No part of this publication may be reproduced, distributed, or transmitted in any form or by any means, including photocopying, recording, or other electronic or mechanical methods, without the prior written permission of the publisher, except in the case of brief quotations embodied in critical reviews and certain other noncommercial uses permitted by copyright law.

The information contained in this book is intended for educational purposes only and is not intended to replace the advice of a professional. The author and publisher have made every effort to ensure the accuracy of the information herein. However, the author and publisher make no representation or warranties with respect to the accuracy or completeness of the contents of this book and specifically disclaim any implied warranties of merchantability or fitness for a particular purpose. The information contained herein is provided on an "as is" basis without warranty of any kind.

The author and publisher shall have no liability or responsibility to any person or entity with respect to any loss or damage caused, or alleged to be caused, directly or indirectly by the information contained in this book.

Trademarks, service marks, and logos appearing in this book are the property of their respective owners. They are used for identification purposes only and not for endorsement, sponsorship, or affiliation.

Foreword

Welcome to the world of veganism, a journey that promises not only a profound transformation in your own life but also a positive impact on the world around you. In the pages of this book, you will find a comprehensive guide to embracing a vegan diet and lifestyle, from understanding the ethical foundations of veganism to mastering essential kitchen skills and exploring delicious plant-based recipes.

Veganism is more than just a dietary choice; it is a compassionate way of life rooted in the belief that all sentient beings deserve respect, freedom, and protection. The chapters in this book delve into the ethical foundations of veganism, exploring concepts like animal rights, nonviolence, and environmental sustainability. You will gain a deeper understanding of the principles that underpin the vegan movement, empowering you to align your actions with your values and make choices that minimize harm.

One of the highlights of this book is the exploration of the health benefits of a vegan diet. You will discover how a plant-based lifestyle can nourish your body and promote overall well-being. From reduced risk of chronic diseases to improved digestion and mental well-being, the positive impact of a vegan diet on your health is truly remarkable. The chapters dedicated to nutrition, meal planning, and kitchen skills will equip you with the knowledge and tools to create balanced and nutrient-rich meals that support your health and vitality.

But this book goes beyond the individual benefits of veganism. It also explores how to navigate social situations, entertain guests, and raise vegan children, ensuring that your vegan journey extends to all aspects of your life. You will find practical tips and inspiring ideas to make veganism a joyful and inclusive experience, whether you are hosting a dinner party or packing a quick and delicious meal for a busy day.

In addition to its emphasis on personal well-being and ethical considerations, this book explores the broader impact of veganism on the planet. You will learn about the environmental sustainability of a plant-based lifestyle and how your choices can contribute to a more sustainable and compassionate world.

Lastly, this book invites you to become an advocate and activist for the vegan cause. It provides insights into effective advocacy strategies, volunteering opportunities, and ways to support animal welfare organizations. By raising your voice and taking action, you can be a catalyst for change and inspire others to join the vegan movement.

The vegan journey is not always easy, but it is undoubtedly rewarding. It is a journey of growth, compassion, and empowerment. As you turn the pages of this book, I encourage you to approach each chapter with an open mind and an open heart. Embrace the knowledge, embrace the challenges, and embrace the incredible potential within you to make a difference.

May this book be your guide and companion as you embark on this transformative journey. Let it ignite your passion for veganism and inspire you to live a life that aligns with your deepest values. Together, we can create a kinder, healthier, and more sustainable world for all beings.

Welcome to the vibrant and compassionate world of veganism!

Summary

Foreword 3

Chapter 1: Understanding Veganism 16

  What is Veganism? 16

  The Ethical Foundations 18

    Animal Rights 18

    Nonviolence and Non-Exploitation 18

    Species Equality 19

    Environmental Sustainability 19

    Intersectionality and Social Justice 19

    Sentience and Consideration 19

    Anti-Speciesism 20

    Minimizing Harm 20

    Personal Integrity and Consistency 20

    Evolving Ethical Consciousness 20

    Ethical Consumerism 21

    Advocacy and Activism 21

  Health Benefits of a Vegan Diet 22

    Nutrient-Dense 22

    Reduced Risk of Chronic Diseases 22

    Heart Health 22

    Weight Management 23

    Improved Digestive Health 23

    Lower Blood Sugar Levels 23

    Enhanced Gut Microbiota 24

    Reduced Inflammation 24

    Lower Risk of Certain Cancers 24

    Improved Kidney Function 24

    Better Blood Sugar Control 25

    Lower Risk of Gallstones 25

    Potential Weight Loss 25

Reduced Risk of Foodborne Illnesses 25

Mental Well-being 26

Improved Skin Health 26

Reduced Risk of Digestive Disorders 26

Lowered Risk of Stroke 27

Decreased Risk of Allergies and Asthma 27

Longevity and Healthy Aging 27

Environmental Impact 29

Chapter 2: Essential Vegan Kitchen Skills 37

Plant-Based Nutrition 37

Macronutrients in a Vegan Diet 46

Carbohydrates: 46

Proteins: 46

Fats: 47

Balancing Macronutrients: 48

Fiber: 49

Omega-3 Fatty Acids: 49

Calorie Considerations: 49

Individualized Needs: 50

Micronutrients and Supplements 52

Vitamin B12 52

Iron 52

Calcium 53

Omega-3 Fatty Acids 53

Vitamin D 53

Iodine 54

Zinc: 54

Vitamin K2 54

Selenium 55

Iodine 55

Vitamin E 55

Vitamin A 56

Vitamin C 56

Magnesium 57

Meal Planning and Balancing Nutritional Needs 59

Variety and Diversity 59

Macronutrient Balance 59

Fiber-Rich Foods 60

Micronutrient-Rich Foods 60

Calcium and Vitamin D 60

Omega-3 Fatty Acids 60

Meal Prep and Batch Cooking 61

Seek Professional Guidance 61

Portion Control 61

Adequate Protein Intake 62

Smart Snacking 62

Hydration 62

Mindful Eating 63

Meal Planning Apps and Websites 63

Flexibility and Experimentation 63

Vegan Sources of Protein, Calcium, Iron, and Omega-3s 65

Chapter 3: Stocking Your Vegan Pantry 70

Essential Ingredients for Vegan Cooking 70

Plant-Based Proteins 70

Nuts and Seeds 71

Plant-Based Milks and Creams 71

Nutritional Yeast 71

Condiments and Flavor Enhancers 72

Fresh Fruits and Vegetables 72

Vegetable Broth and Stock 72

Dried Herbs and Spices 73

Agave Nectar or Maple Syrup 73

Nut Butters 73

Citrus Juices and Zest 73

Tamari or Soy Sauce 74

Canned Tomatoes and Tomato Paste 74

Whole Food Sweeteners 74

Whole Grains and Legumes 75

Plant-Based Milks and Dairy Alternatives 84

Natural Sweeteners and Flavor Enhancers 92

Chapter 4: Mastering Vegan Cooking Techniques 101

Cooking with Tofu and Tempeh 101

Perfecting Vegan Baking 109

Sauteing, Stir-Frying, and Grilling 117

Steaming, Boiling, and Roasting 125

Chapter 5: Special Occasions and Beyond 131

Vegan Entertaining and Party Foods 131

Hosting a Vegan Dinner Party 139

Menu Planning 139

Ingredient Selection 139

Appetizers and Starters 140

Main Course Brilliance 140

Sides and Accompaniments 140

Desserts to Delight 140

Beverage Selection 141

Communication 141

Table Setting and Ambience 141

Enjoy the Experience 141

Interactive Elements 142

Vegan Cheese and Charcuterie Board 142

Seasonal and Local Ingredients: 142

Creative Vegan Cocktails 143

Vegan Cheese and Dessert Tastings 143

Cooking Demonstrations 143

Thoughtful Accommodations 144

Sustainable Tableware 144

Party Favors..144

Post-Dinner Discussion 144

Elegant Appetizers and Finger Foods 146

Refreshing Mocktails and Party Drinks 155

Chapter 6: Vegan on the Go: Quick and Easy Meals 164

Portable Lunch Ideas 164

Travel-Friendly Snacks and Treats...173

Healthy Meals for Busy Weeknights 180

Buddha bowls 183

Zucchini noodles (zoodles) 183

Quick and easy tacos 183

Quinoa or couscous salad 184

Veggie-packed pasta...184

Stuffed bell peppers 184

Omelets or frittatas 184

Prepping and Packing Vegan Meals 186

Use versatile Ingredients: 189

Make use of freezer-friendly options...189

Embrace Mason jar salads 189

Consider snack packs 190

Repurpose leftovers creatively...190

Don't forget about breakfast and snacks 190

Stay organized with a meal prep planner 190

Chapter 7: Veganism for Families and Kids 192

Raising Vegan Children 192

Educate yourself...192

Consult a healthcare professional 192

Ensure a balanced diet 193

Protein sources 193

Calcium and vitamin D 193

Iron-rich foods 193

Omega-3 fatty acids..194

Variety and supplementation 194

Teach and empower 194

Address social situations 194

Monitor growth and development 195

Kid-Friendly Vegan Lunches and Snacks 196

Sandwiches and Wraps... 196

Veggie and Dip Platter 196

Bento Boxes.. 196

Pasta Salad 197

Veggie Sushi Rolls 197

Fruit Kebabs 197

Energy Balls 197

Smoothies... 198

Trail Mix 198

Mini Veggie Pizza 198

Food Shapes and Skewers 199

Mini Pancakes or Waffles 199

Crunchy Snacks.. 199

Fruit Salsa and Cinnamon Tortilla Chips 200

Vegan Yogurt Parfait 200

Veggie Sticks with Hummus Faces 200

Frozen Fruit Pops 200

Veggie Quesadillas 201

Sweet Potato Fries 201

Fruit and Veggie Smoothie Bowls 201

Family-Friendly Dinner Ideas..203

Veggie-loaded Pasta 203

Build-Your-Own Tacos 203

Veggie Stir-Fry 203

Baked Potato Bar 204

Lentil Shepherd's Pie 204

Quinoa and Veggie Stuffed Peppers...204

Veggie Pizza Night.. 204

Chickpea Curry.. 205

Veggie Burgers.. 205

One-Pot Pasta Primavera.. 205

Exploring Veganism with Teens...207

Open Communication 207

Educate Together 207

Involve Teens in Meal Planning 207

Cooking and Culinary Skills.. 208

Encourage Independence 208

Nutritional Awareness 208

Addressing Social Situations 209

Supportive Community 209

Encourage Critical Thinking.. 209

Celebrate Milestones..210

Chapter 8: Vegan for Fitness and Sports Performance 211

Fueling Your Workouts with Plant-Based Foods...211

Pre-Workout Nutrition:...211

Hydration 211

During-Workout Snacks 211

Post-Workout Recovery 212

Protein for Muscle Repair.. 212

Nutrient-Dense Meals... 212

Healthy Fats 213

Timing and Portion Control... 213

Experiment and Listen to Your Body 213

Consider Professional Guidance... 214

Pre- and Post-Workout Nutrition for Vegans 215

Pre-Workout Nutrition 215

Complex Carbohydrates... 215

Protein 215

Minimal Fat... 216

Timing 216

Post-Workout Nutrition: 216

Protein for Muscle Repair 216

Complex Carbohydrates 216

Nutrient-Dense Foods 217

Hydration 217

Timing 217

Balanced Meal or Snack 217

Building Muscle on a Vegan Diet 219

Plant-Based Protein Sources 219

Calorie Surplus 219

Strength Training 220

Post-Workout Nutrition: 220

Meal Planning and Timing 220

Micronutrient Considerations 221

Hydration 221

Rest and Recovery 221

Professional Guidance 221

Progressive Overload 222

Adequate Carbohydrates 222

Healthy Fats 223

Meal Timing 223

Supplement Considerations 223

Patience and Consistency 224

Tracking Progress 224

Listen to Your Body 224

Supportive Community 224

Vegan Athletes and Success Stories 226

Scott Jurek 226

Venus Williams 226

Patrik Baboumian 227

Fiona Oakes 227

Morgan Mitchell 227

Derrick Morgan 227

Tia Blanco 228

Chapter 9: Vegan Beauty and Personal Care 230

Cruelty-Free and Vegan Cosmetics 230

Cruelty-Free Certification 230

Animal-Derived Ingredients: 230

Ethical Testing Methods 231

Plant-Based Ingredients: 231

Environmental Impact 231

Transparency and Labels 232

Market Accessibility 232

Consumer Empowerment 232

Online Resources 233

DIY Vegan Skincare Recipes 234

Cleansing Oils 234

Face Masks 234

Body Scrubs 235

Facial Toners 235

Lip Balms 235

Moisturizers 235

Eye Creams 236

Face Serums 236

Navigating Vegan-Friendly Haircare and Body Products 238

Reading Labels 238

Plant-Based Ingredients: 238

Synthetic Alternatives 239

SLS and SLES-Free 239

Ethical Certification 239

Natural Fragrances 239

Environmentally Conscious Packaging 240

Research and Reviews 240

Brand Transparency 240

Personal Preferences 240

Ethical Fashion: Vegan Clothing and Accessories...........................242

Animal-Free Materials 242

Cruelty-Free Production..242

Sustainable Manufacturing 243

Innovative Materials...243

Fair Trade and Ethical Labor 243

Transparency and Certifications 244

Fashion Forward Designs..244

Consumer Empowerment 244

Accessible and Diverse Options 245

Personal Expression 245

Chapter 10: Vegan Ethics and Activism..246

Understanding Animal Rights and Liberation 246

Effective Advocacy: Speaking Up for Animals.................................250

Getting Involved: Volunteerism and Animal Sanctuaries 253

Making a Difference: Donations and Supporting Animal Welfare Organizations 256

Vegan recipes to delight your palate 259

Breakfast recipes...259

Lunch Recipes...266

Dinner recipes...273

Protein Recipes 281

Dessert...289

Conclusion...296

Chapter 1: Understanding Veganism

What is Veganism?

Veganism is a lifestyle and philosophy that seeks to eliminate the use and exploitation of animals as much as possible. It is a way of living that aims to avoid the consumption of animal products, including meat, fish, dairy, eggs, honey, and other animal-derived ingredients.

At its core, veganism is driven by ethical concerns for animal rights, environmental sustainability, and personal health. People choose to follow a vegan lifestyle for various reasons. Some adopt veganism due to their belief in the inherent value and rights of animals, rejecting the idea that animals should be used for food, clothing, entertainment, or any other human purposes. Others are motivated by the environmental impact of animal agriculture, recognizing that it is a significant contributor to deforestation, greenhouse gas emissions, and water pollution. Additionally, many individuals embrace veganism for health reasons, as research suggests that plant-based diets can be nutritionally adequate and may offer various health benefits, such as reducing the risk of certain chronic diseases.

Vegans strive to make conscious choices that minimize harm to animals, which extends beyond dietary choices. They also avoid using products tested on animals and opt for cruelty-free alternatives in personal care, cosmetics, and household items. Veganism promotes compassion, sustainability, and a more harmonious coexistence with other beings and the planet.

It is important to note that veganism is a personal choice, and individuals may adopt it to varying degrees based on their beliefs, circumstances, and available resources. Some people may choose to gradually transition to a vegan lifestyle, while others may embrace it more strictly from the beginning. Ultimately, veganism is about making conscious decisions aligned with one's values to create a positive impact on animals, the environment, and personal well-being.

The Ethical Foundations

The ethical foundations of veganism are rooted in the belief that all animals have inherent value and deserve to be treated with respect, compassion, and justice. Vegans reject the notion that animals should be treated as mere commodities or resources for human use. They advocate for the ethical consideration of animals, recognizing their capacity to experience pain, pleasure, emotions, and their desire to live free from suffering.

Some key ethical principles that underpin veganism include:

Animal Rights: Veganism acknowledges that animals have their own interests, and their right to life and freedom should be respected. It challenges the use of animals for food, clothing, experimentation, entertainment, or any other purpose that involves their exploitation and harm.

Nonviolence and Non-Exploitation: Vegans promote nonviolence and non-exploitation in their relationships with animals. They reject practices such as factory farming, animal testing, hunting, and other forms of animal exploitation.

Species Equality: Veganism emphasizes the equal moral consideration of all species. It challenges the notion of human superiority over other animals and recognizes that all sentient beings have a right to be free from unnecessary suffering and exploitation.

Environmental Sustainability: The ethical foundations of veganism extend beyond animal welfare and encompass environmental concerns. Animal agriculture is a significant contributor to deforestation, greenhouse gas emissions, water pollution, and other environmental issues. By adopting a plant-based diet, vegans aim to reduce their ecological footprint and contribute to a more sustainable future.

Intersectionality and Social Justice: Veganism recognizes the interconnectedness of various forms of oppression and advocates for social justice. It acknowledges the intersections of animal rights with issues such as human rights, labor rights, and social inequalities, seeking to address the interconnected systems of oppression.

Sentience and Consideration: Veganism acknowledges that animals are sentient beings capable of experiencing pleasure, pain, emotions, and a range of sensations. Vegans believe that sentience itself warrants moral consideration and respect for the well-being of all sentient beings.

Anti-Speciesism: Veganism challenges the concept of speciesism, which is the discrimination or prejudice based on species membership. It rejects the belief that humans are inherently superior to other animals and advocates for equal consideration of interests and rights regardless of species.

Minimizing Harm: Vegans strive to minimize harm to animals as much as possible. They actively seek alternatives to animal-derived products and support industries that prioritize the well-being and rights of animals.

Personal Integrity and Consistency: Adopting veganism is often driven by the desire to live in alignment with one's values and principles. Vegans strive for consistency between their ethical beliefs and daily actions, promoting integrity and moral responsibility.

Evolving Ethical Consciousness: Veganism recognizes that ethical considerations can evolve and expand over time. It encourages ongoing self-reflection, learning, and open-mindedness to deepen understanding and refine ethical choices.

Ethical Consumerism: Veganism extends beyond personal dietary choices and encompasses a broader approach to consumption. Vegans aim to support businesses and industries that align with their ethical values, opting for cruelty-free, sustainable, and ethically produced goods and services.

Advocacy and Activism: Many vegans engage in advocacy and activism to raise awareness about animal rights, promote veganism, and advocate for policy changes that protect animals and the environment. They strive to inspire positive change and challenge societal norms regarding the treatment of animals.

Ultimately, the ethical foundations of veganism center on compassion, justice, respect, and the recognition of the inherent value of all living beings. By embracing veganism, individuals seek to live in harmony with their ethical principles and contribute to a more compassionate and sustainable world for animals and the planet as a whole.

Health Benefits of a Vegan Diet

A vegan diet, when properly planned and balanced, can offer a range of health benefits. These benefits arise from the emphasis on whole plant-based foods and the avoidance of animal products. Here are some of the potential health benefits associated with a vegan diet:

Nutrient-Dense: A well-planned vegan diet can be rich in vitamins, minerals, antioxidants, and fiber. By including a variety of fruits, vegetables, whole grains, legumes, nuts, and seeds, vegans can meet their nutritional needs and promote overall health.

Reduced Risk of Chronic Diseases: Studies have shown that a vegan diet can lower the risk of various chronic diseases. For instance, plant-based diets are associated with a decreased risk of heart disease, high blood pressure, type 2 diabetes, certain types of cancer (such as colorectal cancer), and obesity.

Heart Health: Vegan diets are typically low in saturated fat and cholesterol, which are known to contribute to heart disease.

Instead, they are rich in heart-healthy nutrients, such as fiber, antioxidants, and unsaturated fats (found in foods like nuts, seeds, and avocados), which can help lower blood pressure and improve overall cardiovascular health.

Weight Management: Vegan diets tend to be lower in calorie density and higher in fiber, which can promote satiety and weight management. Additionally, plant-based diets have been associated with lower body mass index (BMI) and reduced risk of obesity.

Improved Digestive Health: The high fiber content of vegan diets can support a healthy digestive system, promoting regular bowel movements and preventing constipation. It may also reduce the risk of conditions like diverticulitis and hemorrhoids.

Lower Blood Sugar Levels: Plant-based diets, particularly those emphasizing whole grains, legumes, and fiber-rich foods, have been shown to improve blood sugar control and insulin sensitivity, making them beneficial for individuals with type 2 diabetes or those at risk of developing it.

Enhanced Gut Microbiota: A vegan diet rich in fiber and plant-based foods can contribute to a diverse and beneficial gut microbiota. A healthy gut microbiome has been linked to improved digestion, immune function, and mental well-being.

Reduced Inflammation: Many plant-based foods are naturally anti-inflammatory, thanks to their high levels of antioxidants and phytochemicals. By reducing inflammation in the body, a vegan diet may help alleviate symptoms of inflammatory conditions, such as arthritis and certain autoimmune diseases.

Lower Risk of Certain Cancers: Plant-based diets have been linked to a reduced risk of certain cancers, including breast, prostate, and colon cancers. The abundance of fiber, antioxidants, and phytochemicals found in plant-based foods may contribute to their protective effects against cancer.

Improved Kidney Function: Vegan diets, particularly those low in animal protein, may help improve kidney function and reduce the risk of developing kidney disease. Plant-based diets tend to be lower in phosphorus and have a more favorable impact on kidney health.

Better Blood Sugar Control: Vegan diets can be beneficial for individuals with type 2 diabetes or those at risk of developing the condition. Plant-based diets, with their emphasis on whole grains, legumes, fruits, and vegetables, can help improve blood sugar control and insulin sensitivity.

Lower Risk of Gallstones: Studies suggest that individuals following a vegan diet have a lower risk of developing gallstones compared to those consuming animal-based diets. The high fiber content of plant-based diets may play a role in reducing gallstone formation.

Potential Weight Loss: Adopting a vegan diet may aid in weight loss or weight management due to the naturally lower calorie density of plant-based foods. Additionally, the emphasis on whole, unprocessed foods and the avoidance of high-fat animal products can contribute to maintaining a healthy weight.

Reduced Risk of Foodborne Illnesses: A vegan diet eliminates the consumption of animal products that are often associated with foodborne illnesses caused by bacteria such as Salmonella, E. coli, and Campylobacter. Therefore, the risk of contracting these illnesses may be lower in individuals following a vegan lifestyle.

Mental Well-being: While more research is needed, some studies suggest that plant-based diets may have a positive impact on mental health. The abundance of nutrients, antioxidants, and anti-inflammatory compounds found in plant-based foods, coupled with the avoidance of processed foods, may contribute to improved mood and mental well-being.

Improved Skin Health: The abundance of antioxidants and nutrient-dense foods in a vegan diet can contribute to healthier skin. A plant-based diet rich in fruits, vegetables, and whole grains provides essential vitamins, minerals, and antioxidants that promote skin health and may reduce the risk of skin conditions like acne and eczema.

Reduced Risk of Digestive Disorders: Vegan diets, particularly those rich in fiber from whole plant-based foods, can help promote a healthy gut microbiome and improve digestive health. Adequate fiber intake supports regular bowel movements, prevents constipation, and may reduce the risk of digestive disorders like diverticulosis and hemorrhoids.

__Lowered Risk of Stroke__: Research suggests that a vegan diet may be associated with a lower risk of stroke. The avoidance of animal products, which are often high in saturated fats and cholesterol, and the inclusion of fiber-rich plant foods can contribute to improved cardiovascular health and a reduced risk of stroke.

__Decreased Risk of Allergies and Asthma__: Some studies indicate that individuals following a vegan diet may have a lower risk of developing allergies and asthma. The avoidance of dairy products, which are common allergens, and the increased consumption of anti-inflammatory plant foods may play a role in this association.

__Longevity and Healthy Aging__: Several studies have suggested that adherence to a plant-based diet may be associated with increased longevity and a reduced risk of age-related diseases. The abundance of antioxidants, anti-inflammatory compounds, and nutrient-dense foods in a vegan diet may contribute to healthy aging and overall longevity.

It's important to note that individual results may vary, and the overall health benefits of a vegan diet can depend on factors such as overall diet quality, lifestyle choices, and individual health conditions. It's recommended to consult with a healthcare professional or registered dietitian to ensure a well-planned and balanced vegan diet that meets individual nutritional needs.

Environmental Impact

The concept of environmental impact refers to the effects human activities have on the natural world, including ecosystems, biodiversity, and natural resources. In the context of veganism, adopting a plant-based diet can significantly reduce an individual's environmental footprint and contribute to a more sustainable future.

Animal agriculture, particularly industrialized factory farming, is a major contributor to environmental degradation. It has significant implications for climate change, deforestation, water usage, and pollution. The production of animal-based foods requires vast amounts of land, water, and resources, while also generating substantial greenhouse gas emissions.

By choosing a vegan lifestyle, individuals can help mitigate these environmental challenges. Plant-based diets require fewer resources and have a lower carbon footprint compared to diets rich in animal products. The cultivation of plant foods, such as fruits, vegetables, grains, and legumes, generally requires less land, water, and energy. It helps conserve natural habitats, reduces deforestation, and mitigates soil erosion.

In addition, the livestock sector is responsible for a significant portion of global greenhouse gas emissions, primarily in the form of methane and nitrous oxide. Methane, emitted by cattle and other ruminant animals, has a much higher global warming potential than carbon dioxide. By reducing or eliminating the consumption of animal products, individuals can effectively decrease their personal carbon footprint and contribute to efforts aimed at combating climate change.

Water usage is another critical environmental concern. Animal agriculture is a water-intensive industry, requiring vast amounts of water for animal hydration, feed crops, and processing. By opting for a plant-based diet, individuals can conserve water resources, as plant foods generally have lower water requirements compared to animal products.

Moreover, the production of animal-based foods contributes to water pollution through the discharge of animal waste and the use of chemical fertilizers and pesticides. By reducing reliance on animal agriculture, individuals can help minimize water pollution and protect aquatic ecosystems.

Adopting a vegan lifestyle also aligns with principles of biodiversity conservation. Animal agriculture often involves clearing land for livestock grazing or feed crop production, leading to habitat destruction and loss of biodiversity. By reducing demand for animal products, individuals can contribute to the preservation of ecosystems and the protection of endangered species.

The concept of environmental impact encompasses the consequences of human activities on the natural world, including ecosystems, biodiversity, and natural resources. In the context of veganism, adopting a plant-based diet emerges as a compelling solution to mitigate these impacts and promote environmental sustainability.

Animal agriculture, particularly in the form of intensive factory farming, exerts substantial pressure on the environment. This industry significantly contributes to climate change, deforestation, water scarcity, and pollution. The production of animal-based foods necessitates vast amounts of land, water, and resources, while simultaneously releasing significant greenhouse gas emissions.

By embracing a vegan lifestyle, individuals can actively address these environmental challenges. Plant-based diets require fewer resources and have a lower carbon footprint compared to diets centered around animal products. The cultivation of plant foods, including fruits, vegetables, grains, and legumes, generally demands less land, water, and energy. By opting for these options, individuals contribute to the conservation of natural habitats, mitigating deforestation, and curtailing soil erosion.

Moreover, the livestock sector constitutes a substantial source of global greenhouse gas emissions, primarily methane and nitrous oxide. Methane, in particular, possesses a significantly higher global warming potential than carbon dioxide. Through the reduction or elimination of animal products, individuals can effectively diminish their personal carbon footprint and actively support endeavors combatting climate change.

Water usage stands as another critical environmental concern. Animal agriculture necessitates large quantities of water for animal hydration, feed crops, and processing. By transitioning to a plant-based diet, individuals can conserve water resources, given that plant foods typically require less water compared to animal products.

Furthermore, the production of animal-based foods often leads to water pollution through the discharge of animal waste and the application of chemical fertilizers and pesticides. By reducing reliance on animal agriculture, individuals can help minimize water pollution, safeguarding aquatic ecosystems and their inhabitants.

Adopting a vegan lifestyle also aligns with the principles of biodiversity conservation. Animal agriculture frequently involves land clearance for livestock grazing or the cultivation of feed crops, resulting in habitat destruction and biodiversity loss. By diminishing the demand for animal products, individuals actively contribute to the preservation of ecosystems and the protection of endangered species.

The concept of environmental impact revolves around the consequences of human activities on the natural world, encompassing ecosystems, biodiversity, and natural resources. Within the realm of veganism, adopting a plant-based diet emerges as a powerful catalyst to mitigate these impacts and foster environmental sustainability.

Animal agriculture, particularly in the form of intensive factory farming, exerts immense pressure on the environment. This industry significantly contributes to climate change, deforestation, water scarcity, and pollution. The production of animal-based foods demands vast quantities of land, water, and resources, concurrently releasing substantial greenhouse gas emissions.

By embracing a vegan lifestyle, individuals can proactively address these environmental challenges. Plant-based diets require fewer resources and boast a lower carbon footprint compared to diets centered around animal products. The cultivation of plant foods—fruits, vegetables, grains, and legumes—generally necessitates less land, water, and energy. By choosing these options, individuals contribute to the conservation of natural habitats, mitigating deforestation, and curtailing soil erosion.

Moreover, the livestock sector constitutes a significant source of global greenhouse gas emissions, particularly methane and nitrous oxide. Methane, with its heightened global warming potential compared to carbon dioxide, poses a particularly potent threat. Through the reduction or elimination of animal products, individuals can effectively diminish their personal carbon footprint and actively support endeavors combatting climate change.

Water usage stands as another pivotal environmental concern. Animal agriculture requires substantial volumes of water for animal hydration, feed crops, and processing. Transitioning to a plant-based diet enables individuals to conserve water resources, as plant foods typically necessitate less water compared to animal products.

Furthermore, the production of animal-based foods often leads to water pollution through the discharge of animal waste and the application of chemical fertilizers and pesticides. By reducing reliance on animal agriculture, individuals contribute to minimizing water pollution, safeguarding aquatic ecosystems and their inhabitants.

Adopting a vegan lifestyle also aligns with the principles of biodiversity conservation. Animal agriculture frequently entails land clearance for livestock grazing or the cultivation of feed crops, resulting in habitat destruction and biodiversity loss. Diminishing the demand for animal products actively contributes to the preservation of ecosystems and the protection of endangered species.

In conclusion, embracing a vegan lifestyle offers a comprehensive and seamless approach to address environmental concerns. Opting for plant-based diets enables individuals to combat climate change, conserve water resources, protect biodiversity, and reduce pollution. Veganism serves as a catalyst for positive change, fostering a harmonious and sustainable future for the planet and all its inhabitants.

Chapter 2: Essential Vegan Kitchen Skills

Plant-Based Nutrition

Plant-based nutrition refers to a dietary approach that centers around whole plant foods while minimizing or excluding animal products. It emphasizes the consumption of fruits, vegetables, grains, legumes, nuts, and seeds as the foundation of a well-balanced diet. By embracing plant-based nutrition, individuals can enjoy a wide array of health benefits while promoting sustainable food choices.

At the core of plant-based nutrition is the recognition that plants offer an abundance of essential nutrients, including vitamins, minerals, antioxidants, and fiber. Fruits and vegetables provide a colorful array of vitamins such as vitamin C, vitamin A, and various B vitamins, along with minerals like potassium and magnesium. These nutrients are vital for overall health and play key roles in supporting the immune system, promoting healthy skin, and ensuring proper organ function.

Whole grains, such as quinoa, brown rice, and whole wheat, are rich in complex carbohydrates, fiber, and important minerals like iron and zinc. They provide sustained energy, promote digestive health, and contribute to feelings of satiety.

Legumes, including beans, lentils, and chickpeas, are excellent sources of plant-based protein, fiber, iron, and other essential nutrients. They are not only versatile in cooking but also contribute to heart health, blood sugar control, and weight management.

Nuts and seeds offer a plethora of healthy fats, protein, fiber, vitamins, and minerals. They are particularly rich in omega-3 fatty acids, which are important for brain health, heart health, and reducing inflammation. Chia seeds, flaxseeds, and walnuts are notable sources of these beneficial fats.

Plant-based nutrition also emphasizes the importance of adequate calcium, which can be obtained from plant sources such as fortified plant milks, tofu, leafy greens (like kale and broccoli), and sesame seeds. Iron, another essential nutrient, can be obtained from plant foods such as lentils, spinach, and fortified cereals. Plant-based sources of protein include tofu, tempeh, seitan, legumes, and quinoa.

A well-planned plant-based diet can meet all the nutritional requirements at various stages of life, from infancy to adulthood. However, it's important to ensure adequate intake of certain nutrients that may require special attention in a plant-based diet, such as vitamin B12, vitamin D, and omega-3 fatty acids. Supplementation or fortified foods may be necessary to ensure sufficient levels of these nutrients.

In addition to the numerous health benefits, embracing plant-based nutrition aligns with principles of sustainability, as plant foods generally require fewer resources and have a lower environmental impact compared to animal-based products. This dietary approach promotes a balanced and diverse intake of plant foods, enabling individuals to nourish their bodies while contributing to a healthier planet.

Plant-based nutrition encompasses a dietary approach that revolves around the consumption of predominantly whole plant foods while minimizing or excluding animal products. It emphasizes the central role of fruits, vegetables, grains, legumes, nuts, and seeds as the foundation of a well-balanced diet. By embracing plant-based nutrition, individuals can unlock a wealth of health benefits while contributing to a sustainable and ethical food system.

At its core, plant-based nutrition recognizes the inherent nutritional value of plants, which offer an abundance of essential nutrients required for optimal health. Fruits and vegetables provide a vibrant spectrum of vitamins, including vitamin C, vitamin A, and various B vitamins, along with an array of minerals such as potassium, magnesium, and folate. These nutrients are crucial for supporting the immune system, promoting healthy cell function, and fueling overall vitality.

Whole grains, such as quinoa, brown rice, and whole wheat products, form a significant part of a plant-based diet. These grains are rich in complex carbohydrates, dietary fiber, and important minerals like iron and zinc. They provide sustained energy, promote healthy digestion, and contribute to feelings of satiety and overall well-being.

Legumes, encompassing beans, lentils, and chickpeas, are nutritional powerhouses in the plant-based diet. They offer a remarkable combination of plant-based protein, dietary fiber, iron, and various other essential nutrients. Legumes are not only versatile and affordable but also play a vital role in supporting heart health, blood sugar control, and weight management.

Nuts and seeds add a delightful crunch to the plant-based plate while offering a range of health benefits. They are rich in healthy fats, protein, dietary fiber, vitamins, and minerals. Almonds, flaxseeds, chia seeds, and walnuts are notable examples, providing essential omega-3 fatty acids that support brain health, cardiovascular well-being, and inflammation reduction.

Calcium, a crucial mineral for bone health, can be obtained from plant-based sources such as fortified plant milks, tofu, leafy greens (like kale and broccoli), and sesame seeds. Iron, another vital nutrient, can be sourced from plant foods like lentils, spinach, and fortified cereals. Plant-based protein sources include tofu, tempeh, seitan, legumes, and quinoa, providing ample options for meeting daily protein needs.

While plant-based nutrition can provide a well-rounded and nutrient-dense diet, special attention should be given to certain nutrients that may require additional consideration, such as vitamin B12, vitamin D, and omega-3 fatty acids. These can be obtained through fortified foods or dietary supplements to ensure optimal nutritional status.

Beyond the individual benefits, embracing plant-based nutrition aligns with principles of sustainability and ethical food choices. Plant foods generally require fewer resources and have a lower environmental impact compared to animal-based products. By adopting a plant-based diet, individuals contribute to reducing greenhouse gas emissions, preserving land and water resources, and promoting a more compassionate and sustainable food system.

Plant-based nutrition is a dietary approach centered around consuming primarily whole plant foods while minimizing or excluding animal products. It emphasizes the importance of fruits, vegetables, grains, legumes, nuts, and seeds as the cornerstone of a well-rounded diet. By adopting plant-based nutrition, individuals can reap a plethora of health benefits while promoting sustainable and ethical food choices.

At its core, plant-based nutrition recognizes the inherent nutritional value of plants, which are rich sources of essential nutrients. Fruits and vegetables offer a vibrant array of vitamins, including vitamin C, vitamin A, and various B vitamins, along with a diverse range of minerals such as potassium, magnesium, and folate. These nutrients play crucial roles in supporting immune function, promoting healthy cell growth and repair, and fueling overall vitality.

Whole grains, such as quinoa, brown rice, and whole wheat, constitute a significant portion of a plant-based diet. These grains provide complex carbohydrates, dietary fiber, and essential minerals like iron and zinc. They supply sustained energy, promote healthy digestion, and contribute to feelings of satiety and overall well-being.

Legumes, including beans, lentils, and chickpeas, are nutritional powerhouses within the plant-based diet. They are rich sources of plant-based protein, dietary fiber, iron, and numerous other essential nutrients. Legumes are versatile, cost-effective, and play pivotal roles in supporting heart health, blood sugar control, and weight management.

Nuts and seeds offer both nutritional value and delightful flavors to the plant-based plate. They provide healthy fats, protein, dietary fiber, vitamins, and minerals. Examples like almonds, flaxseeds, chia seeds, and walnuts are renowned for their omega-3 fatty acid content, which supports brain health, cardiovascular well-being, and inflammation reduction.

Plant-based sources of calcium, a vital mineral for bone health, include fortified plant milks, tofu, leafy greens such as kale and broccoli, and sesame seeds. Iron, another critical nutrient, can be obtained from plant foods like lentils, spinach, and fortified cereals. Protein needs can be met through plant-based sources such as tofu, tempeh, seitan, legumes, and quinoa, offering a diverse range of options.

While plant-based nutrition can provide a well-balanced and nutrient-rich diet, certain nutrients require special attention, such as vitamin B12, vitamin D, and omega-3 fatty acids. These can be obtained through fortified foods or supplements to ensure optimal nutritional status.

Beyond personal health, embracing plant-based nutrition aligns with principles of sustainability and ethical food choices. Plant foods generally require fewer resources and have a lower environmental impact compared to animal-based products. By adopting a plant-based diet, individuals contribute to reducing greenhouse gas emissions, conserving land and water resources, and promoting a more compassionate and sustainable food system.

In conclusion, plant-based nutrition offers a harmonious and health-promoting dietary approach. By prioritizing whole plant foods, individuals can access a wide array of essential nutrients while enjoying the myriad benefits associated with this lifestyle. Embracing plant-based nutrition not only nourishes the body but also supports a sustainable future for ourselves and the planet we inhabit.

Macronutrients in a Vegan Diet

A well-planned vegan diet can provide all the necessary macronutrients—carbohydrates, proteins, and fats—that are essential for a healthy and balanced diet. Here's an overview of macronutrients in a vegan diet:

Carbohydrates:

Carbohydrates are a primary source of energy for the body. They are found abundantly in plant-based foods such as fruits, vegetables, whole grains, legumes, and starchy vegetables. These foods provide complex carbohydrates, which are digested more slowly and provide a steady release of energy. They also supply dietary fiber, which aids in digestion and helps maintain stable blood sugar levels. Examples of vegan carbohydrate sources include brown rice, quinoa, oats, sweet potatoes, lentils, beans, and various fruits and vegetables.

Proteins:

Proteins are essential for various bodily functions, including tissue repair, hormone production, and immune system support. While animal products are rich in protein, a well-planned vegan diet can meet protein needs through plant-based sources. Legumes (such as beans, lentils, and chickpeas), soy products (tofu, tempeh, edamame), seitan, quinoa, nuts, and seeds are excellent vegan protein sources. Combining different plant protein sources throughout the day can ensure a complete amino acid profile, although this need not be achieved at every meal.

Fats:

Fats are vital for energy, nutrient absorption, hormone production, and cell function. Including sources of healthy fats in a vegan diet is important. Plant-based sources of healthy fats include avocados, nuts (such as almonds, walnuts, and cashews), seeds (flaxseeds, chia seeds, and hemp seeds), olives, and oils (such as olive oil, coconut oil, and avocado oil). It's important to consume fats in moderation due to their high calorie content, but incorporating a variety of healthy fats can help meet dietary fat requirements.

It's worth noting that while carbohydrates and proteins offer about 4 calories per gram, fats provide around 9 calories per gram. This higher caloric density of fats can impact overall calorie intake and should be considered when planning a vegan diet for weight management.

In addition to these macronutrients, a well-planned vegan diet should also include an adequate intake of micronutrients, such as vitamins and minerals. Paying attention to nutrients like vitamin B12, iron, calcium, omega-3 fatty acids, iodine, and vitamin D is important for maintaining optimal health. Some of these nutrients may require supplementation or careful food choices, especially since they are less prevalent in plant-based foods.

Balancing Macronutrients:

A well-planned vegan diet should focus on consuming a balance of macronutrients. While the specific ratio of carbohydrates, proteins, and fats can vary depending on individual needs, a general guideline is to aim for approximately 45-65% of daily calories from carbohydrates, 10-35% from protein, and 20-35% from fats. However, these ranges can be adjusted based on personal preferences, activity level, and specific health goals.

It's important to note that individual nutrient needs may vary based on factors such as age, sex, activity level, and overall health. It's advisable to consult with a registered dietitian or healthcare professional to create a personalized nutrition plan that meets individual macronutrient requirements and ensures optimal health.

Fiber:

Fiber is a type of carbohydrate that is indigestible by the human body. It plays a crucial role in digestive health, regulating bowel movements, and promoting feelings of fullness. Whole plant-based foods are naturally rich in fiber, including fruits, vegetables, whole grains, legumes, nuts, and seeds. Consuming an adequate amount of fiber can help maintain a healthy weight, support heart health, and reduce the risk of certain diseases such as type 2 diabetes and colorectal cancer.

Omega-3 Fatty Acids:

Omega-3 fatty acids are a type of polyunsaturated fat that is important for brain health, heart health, and reducing inflammation in the body. While fatty fish is a common source of omega-3s, vegans can obtain these essential fats from plant-based sources. Foods like flaxseeds, chia seeds, hemp seeds, walnuts, and algae-based supplements are excellent sources of omega-3 fatty acids. Including these foods regularly in a vegan diet ensures an adequate intake of these beneficial fats.

Calorie Considerations:

Macronutrients contribute to the overall calorie content of a diet. It's important to be mindful of calorie intake to maintain a healthy weight. While plant-based diets are generally associated with a lower calorie density due to their high fiber and water content, it's still important to pay attention to portion sizes and overall energy balance. Consuming a variety of whole plant foods, including fruits, vegetables, whole grains, legumes, nuts, and seeds, while being mindful of portion sizes, can help achieve a healthy balance of macronutrients and control calorie intake.

Individualized Needs:

It's worth noting that individual macronutrient needs can vary based on factors such as age, sex, activity level, metabolic rate, and specific health goals. Some individuals, such as athletes or those with certain medical conditions, may require adjustments to their macronutrient intake. Consulting with a registered dietitian or healthcare professional who specializes in vegan nutrition can provide personalized guidance based on individual needs and goals.

By embracing a well-planned vegan diet that encompasses a variety of whole plant-based foods and considers individual macronutrient needs, individuals can meet their nutritional requirements and enjoy the many health benefits associated with this dietary approach. A balanced intake of carbohydrates, proteins, fats, fiber, and other essential nutrients can support overall health and well-being while aligning with ethical and sustainable food choices.

Micronutrients and Supplements

Micronutrients are essential vitamins and minerals required by the body in small amounts to support various physiological functions. While a well-planned vegan diet can provide many of these micronutrients, some may require special attention to ensure adequate intake. Here are some key micronutrients in a vegan diet and considerations for supplementation:

Vitamin B12: Vitamin B12 is primarily found in animal-derived foods, and deficiency can occur in vegan diets. It is crucial for nerve function and the production of red blood cells. Vegans should consider taking a vitamin B12 supplement or consuming fortified foods, such as plant-based milks, breakfast cereals, and nutritional yeast, to meet their needs.

Iron: Plant-based sources of iron, known as non-heme iron, are less readily absorbed by the body compared to heme iron found in animal products. However, consuming iron-rich plant foods like legumes, fortified cereals, tofu, nuts, and seeds alongside vitamin C-rich foods can enhance absorption. Iron supplementation may be necessary for individuals with low iron levels or increased iron requirements.

Calcium: While dairy products are a common calcium source, vegans can obtain calcium from plant-based foods such as fortified plant milks, tofu, tempeh, leafy greens (e.g., kale, collard greens), and calcium-set tofu. Calcium absorption can be enhanced by adequate vitamin D levels, regular weight-bearing exercise, and limiting excessive caffeine and sodium intake. Calcium supplementation may be considered if dietary intake is insufficient.

Omega-3 Fatty Acids: While omega-3 fatty acids can be obtained from plant sources like flaxseeds, chia seeds, hemp seeds, and walnuts, they are not in the form of the most biologically active omega-3s, EPA and DHA. Vegans can consider consuming algae-based omega-3 supplements to ensure adequate intake of these essential fats.

Vitamin D: Vitamin D can be synthesized by the body through sunlight exposure, but it can be challenging to obtain enough sunlight, especially in certain regions and during winter months. Vegans should consider getting their vitamin D levels checked and may require supplementation if their levels are low.

Iodine: Iodine is essential for thyroid function and can be obtained from iodized salt or seaweed. However, the iodine content in plant foods can vary, and soil levels can impact iodine content. Vegans should ensure adequate iodine intake through iodized salt or iodine-containing supplements if necessary.

While supplements can be helpful, they should not be seen as a replacement for a well-balanced diet. Emphasizing a diverse range of whole plant-based foods and paying attention to individual micronutrient needs can support optimal nutrition in a vegan diet.

Zinc: Zinc is involved in various enzymatic reactions and plays a crucial role in immune function, wound healing, and DNA synthesis. Plant-based sources of zinc include legumes, whole grains, nuts, and seeds. However, the bioavailability of zinc from plant foods may be lower compared to animal-based sources. Vegans can ensure sufficient zinc intake by consuming a variety of zinc-rich plant foods or considering zinc supplements if necessary.

Vitamin K2: Vitamin K2 is involved in bone health and may have cardiovascular benefits. While plant-based diets can provide vitamin K1 found in leafy green vegetables, fermented foods like natto and certain cheeses are sources of vitamin K2. Vegans may consider vitamin K2 supplements derived from fermented plant-based sources or consult with a healthcare professional for guidance.

Selenium: Selenium is an essential mineral that acts as an antioxidant and supports thyroid function. Plant-based sources of selenium include Brazil nuts, legumes, whole grains, and seeds. The selenium content in plant foods can vary based on soil levels. Vegans should ensure adequate selenium intake through food sources or consider selenium supplements if necessary.

Iodine: Iodine is vital for proper thyroid function and is found in iodized salt, seaweed, and some plant foods depending on soil levels. Vegans who do not consume iodized salt or seaweed regularly should consider monitoring their iodine levels and may need iodine supplements if intake is insufficient.

Vitamin E: Vitamin E is an antioxidant that helps protect cells from damage. It is found in plant-based oils, nuts, seeds, and whole grains. Most individuals consuming a well-balanced vegan diet can obtain sufficient vitamin E through food sources alone, but those with specific needs or limited dietary variety may consider vitamin E supplements.

Remember, individual micronutrient needs can vary based on factors such as age, sex, overall health, and dietary intake. It's advisable to consult with a registered dietitian or healthcare professional who specializes in vegan nutrition to assess specific micronutrient requirements and determine the need for supplementation.

Vitamin A: Vitamin A is essential for vision, immune function, and cell growth. While animal-based products like liver and dairy are rich sources of preformed vitamin A (retinol), plant-based sources provide beta-carotene, which the body converts into vitamin A. Vegan sources of beta-carotene include orange and yellow fruits and vegetables like carrots, sweet potatoes, and mangoes. Vegans can meet their vitamin A needs through these plant sources, but if there are concerns about sufficient intake, a healthcare professional may recommend a vitamin A supplement.

Vitamin C: Vitamin C is an antioxidant that supports immune function, collagen synthesis, and iron absorption. It is plentiful in fruits and vegetables such as citrus fruits, berries, peppers, and leafy greens. A well-rounded vegan diet typically provides adequate vitamin C without the need for supplementation. However, if there are specific concerns or limited fruit and vegetable intake, a vitamin C supplement may be recommended.

Magnesium: Magnesium is involved in over 300 biochemical reactions in the body, including energy production, muscle function, and bone health. Plant-based sources of magnesium include leafy greens, legumes, nuts, seeds, and whole grains. A varied vegan diet can provide sufficient magnesium, but individuals with specific health conditions or limited intake may require magnesium supplements.

It's important to emphasize that supplementation should be personalized and based on individual needs. A balanced vegan diet that includes a wide variety of whole plant-based foods can provide a wealth of micronutrients. However, in some cases, certain individuals may benefit from targeted supplementation to ensure optimal nutrient status. Regular monitoring of nutrient levels through blood tests can help identify any deficiencies and guide supplementation decisions.

It's advisable to consult with a registered dietitian or healthcare professional who specializes in vegan nutrition to assess specific micronutrient requirements and determine the need for supplementation. They can provide personalized guidance based on individual health goals, dietary intake, and potential nutrient gaps. By combining a well-planned vegan diet with appropriate supplementation, individuals can optimize their nutritional status and support overall health and well-being.

Meal Planning and Balancing Nutritional Needs

Meal planning and balancing nutritional needs are essential components of a healthy and well-rounded vegan diet. Here are some key tips and considerations to help you in this process:

Variety and Diversity: Aim for a wide range of plant-based foods to ensure you get a diverse array of nutrients. Include different types of fruits, vegetables, whole grains, legumes, nuts, and seeds in your meals. Each food group offers a unique set of vitamins, minerals, and antioxidants, so incorporating variety ensures a well-rounded nutrient intake.

Macronutrient Balance: Pay attention to the balance of carbohydrates, proteins, and fats in your meals. Include a source of carbohydrates (such as whole grains, fruits, or starchy vegetables), plant-based proteins (like legumes, tofu, tempeh, or seitan), and healthy fats (found in nuts, seeds, avocados, and plant oils) in each meal. Balancing these macronutrients helps provide sustained energy, supports muscle growth and repair, and aids in nutrient absorption.

Fiber-Rich Foods: Plant-based diets are naturally rich in dietary fiber, which promotes digestive health, helps maintain a healthy weight, and supports overall well-being. Include plenty of fiber-rich foods like whole grains, legumes, fruits, vegetables, and nuts/seeds. Aim for a minimum of 25-30 grams of fiber per day.

Micronutrient-Rich Foods: Incorporate foods that are particularly rich in specific micronutrients to meet your nutritional needs. For example, leafy greens like spinach and kale provide iron and calcium, while citrus fruits and berries offer vitamin C. Including a variety of colorful fruits and vegetables ensures a good intake of various vitamins, minerals, and antioxidants.

Calcium and Vitamin D: While plant-based sources of calcium include leafy greens, fortified plant milks, tofu, and sesame seeds, consider calcium and vitamin D supplementation if your intake is inadequate. These nutrients are crucial for bone health, and vitamin D supports calcium absorption. Regular sunlight exposure is also beneficial for vitamin D synthesis.

Omega-3 Fatty Acids: Incorporate plant-based sources of omega-3 fatty acids, such as flaxseeds, chia seeds, hemp seeds, and walnuts, into your meals. If needed, consider algae-based omega-3 supplements to ensure an adequate intake of EPA and DHA, especially for individuals who do not regularly consume these plant sources.

Meal Prep and Batch Cooking: Plan your meals and prep ingredients in advance to make healthy choices more convenient. Cook larger batches of grains, beans, or vegetable dishes that can be portioned and stored for later use. This saves time and ensures you have nutritious meals readily available.

Seek Professional Guidance: Consulting with a registered dietitian or nutritionist who specializes in vegan nutrition can provide personalized guidance tailored to your specific needs and goals. They can help assess your nutrient intake, address any concerns or deficiencies, and create a well-balanced meal plan that meets your nutritional requirements.

Portion Control: While a plant-based diet can be nutrient-dense, portion control is still important to maintain a healthy weight and ensure balanced meals. Be mindful of portion sizes, especially for calorie-dense foods like nuts, seeds, and oils. Use measuring cups, food scales, or visual cues to help estimate appropriate portions.

Adequate Protein Intake: Ensure you include sufficient plant-based protein sources in your meals to meet your daily protein needs. Combining different protein sources throughout the day, such as legumes with whole grains or nuts/seeds with leafy greens, can provide a complete range of essential amino acids. Including protein-rich foods at each meal helps promote satiety and supports muscle maintenance and repair.

Smart Snacking: Plan healthy snacks to keep you satisfied between meals. Opt for whole foods like fresh fruit, raw vegetables with hummus, nuts and seeds, or homemade energy bars. Be mindful of portion sizes to maintain overall calorie balance.

Hydration: Stay adequately hydrated by drinking water throughout the day. Hydration is important for overall health and supports various bodily functions. Consider infusing water with fresh fruits or herbs to add flavor and make it more enjoyable.

Mindful Eating: Practice mindful eating by paying attention to your body's hunger and fullness cues. Eat slowly, savor each bite, and listen to your body's signals of satisfaction. This can help prevent overeating and promote a healthier relationship with food.

Meal Planning Apps and Websites: Utilize meal planning apps and websites that offer vegan recipes and customizable meal plans. These resources can help you discover new recipe ideas, streamline your shopping list, and ensure you have a variety of nutritious meals throughout the week.

Flexibility and Experimentation: Don't be afraid to try new foods and experiment with different flavors and cooking techniques. Embrace the flexibility of a vegan diet by incorporating a wide range of plant-based ingredients into your meals. This helps keep meals interesting, enjoyable, and nutritionally diverse.

Remember, everyone's nutritional needs may vary based on factors such as age, sex, activity level, and health status. Consulting with a registered dietitian or nutritionist who specializes in vegan nutrition can provide personalized guidance and help you tailor your meal planning to meet your specific needs and goals.

By incorporating these tips into your meal planning routine, you can create balanced and nourishing meals that support optimal health and well-being on a vegan diet.

Vegan Sources of Protein, Calcium, Iron, and Omega-3s

A well-planned vegan diet can provide ample sources of protein, calcium, iron, and omega-3 fatty acids. Let's explore these essential nutrients and the plant-based foods that can supply them, creating a smooth and flowing description:

Protein is crucial for various bodily functions, including muscle maintenance and repair, hormone production, and immune support. Vegan sources of protein abound and include legumes like beans, lentils, and chickpeas. These versatile legumes can be incorporated into soups, stews, salads, and even homemade veggie burgers. Other excellent plant-based protein sources include tofu, tempeh, and edamame, which are derived from soybeans. Nuts and seeds, such as almonds, walnuts, chia seeds, and hemp seeds, are also rich in protein. Additionally, whole grains like quinoa, brown rice, and oats contribute to protein intake while offering valuable fiber and other nutrients.

Calcium is essential for strong bones and teeth, nerve function, and muscle contraction. Many plant-based foods can supply calcium. Leafy greens such as kale, collard greens, and spinach are excellent sources. Other calcium-rich vegan options include fortified plant milks like soy milk and almond milk, fortified orange juice, and calcium-set tofu. Sesame seeds and tahini, made from ground sesame seeds, are also good sources of calcium. Incorporating these foods into your diet regularly ensures adequate calcium intake without relying on dairy products.

Iron is vital for oxygen transport and the production of red blood cells. Plant-based sources of iron, known as non-heme iron, are abundant. Legumes like lentils, kidney beans, and chickpeas are excellent iron sources. Dark leafy greens, such as spinach and Swiss chard, are also iron-rich. Including vitamin C-rich foods like citrus fruits, strawberries, and bell peppers alongside iron-rich foods enhances iron absorption. Additionally, fortified breakfast cereals and whole grains like quinoa and amaranth contribute to iron intake.

Omega-3 fatty acids are essential fats that play a crucial role in brain health, heart health, and reducing inflammation. While fatty fish is a common source of omega-3s, vegans can obtain these fatty acids from plant-based sources. Flaxseeds and chia seeds are rich in alpha-linolenic acid (ALA), a type of omega-3 fatty acid. These seeds can be sprinkled on cereals, yogurt alternatives, or incorporated into smoothies. Walnuts are also a good source of omega-3s. For those seeking an additional omega-3 boost, algae-based supplements provide EPA and DHA, the long-chain omega-3s found in fish.

A well-planned vegan diet offers numerous plant-based sources of protein, calcium, iron, and omega-3 fatty acids. These essential nutrients are readily available in a variety of delicious plant foods, allowing you to meet your nutritional needs while following a vegan lifestyle.

Protein is vital for muscle growth and repair, as well as supporting various bodily functions. Legumes, such as beans, lentils, and chickpeas, are excellent sources of plant-based protein. They are versatile ingredients that can be incorporated into soups, stews, salads, and even homemade veggie burgers. Tofu, tempeh, and edamame, which are derived from soybeans, are also rich sources of protein. Nuts and seeds, such as almonds, walnuts, chia seeds, and hemp seeds, not only provide protein but also offer beneficial fats and other important nutrients. Whole grains like quinoa, brown rice, and oats contribute to protein intake while offering valuable fiber and additional nutrients.

Calcium is essential for strong bones and teeth, nerve function, and muscle contraction. Leafy greens like kale, collard greens, and spinach are excellent plant-based sources of calcium. They can be incorporated into salads, smoothies, or cooked dishes. Fortified plant milks, such as soy milk and almond milk, are also calcium-rich options that can be enjoyed on their own or used in recipes. Calcium-set tofu and calcium-fortified orange juice are additional sources to consider. Sesame seeds and tahini, made from ground sesame seeds, are tasty additions to meals and offer a good amount of calcium.

Iron is crucial for oxygen transport and the production of red blood cells. Plant-based sources of iron, known as non-heme iron, are abundant. Legumes like lentils, kidney beans, and chickpeas are excellent sources of iron, along with their protein content. Dark leafy greens like spinach and Swiss chard not only provide iron but also offer other valuable nutrients. It's important to enhance iron absorption by including vitamin C-rich foods like citrus fruits, strawberries, and bell peppers in your meals. Fortified breakfast cereals and whole grains like quinoa and amaranth can also contribute to your iron intake.

Omega-3 fatty acids are essential fats that support brain health, heart health, and reduce inflammation. While fatty fish is a common source of omega-3s, plant-based alternatives exist. Flaxseeds and chia seeds are rich in alpha-linolenic acid (ALA), a type of omega-3 fatty acid. These seeds can be easily incorporated into your diet by sprinkling them on cereals, yogurt alternatives, or blending them into smoothies. Walnuts are another source of omega-3s and can be enjoyed as a snack or added to various dishes. For those looking for an additional omega-3 boost, algae-based supplements are available, providing EPA and DHA, the long-chain omega-3s found in fish.

By incorporating these plant-based protein, calcium, iron, and omega-3 sources into your vegan diet, you can easily meet your nutritional needs. Embracing a wide variety of plant foods ensures a balanced intake of essential nutrients, while offering a wealth of health benefits associated with a vegan lifestyle. Remember to enjoy a diverse range of foods, experiment with different recipes, and consult with a registered dietitian or nutritionist for personalized guidance on optimizing your nutrient intake as a vegan.

Chapter 3: Stocking Your Vegan Pantry

Essential Ingredients for Vegan Cooking

Certainly! Here's a flowing and continuous explanation of essential ingredients for vegan cooking:

When it comes to vegan cooking, a well-stocked pantry with essential ingredients is key to creating delicious and satisfying plant-based meals. These ingredients provide flavor, texture, and versatility, allowing you to craft a wide range of dishes. Let's explore some essential ingredients for vegan cooking:

Plant-Based Proteins: Legumes like beans, lentils, and chickpeas are versatile and protein-rich ingredients that serve as the foundation for many vegan dishes. They can be used in stews, soups, curries, and salads. Tofu and tempeh, derived from soybeans, offer a variety of textures and can be marinated, grilled, stir-fried, or baked. Seitan, made from wheat gluten, is a popular meat substitute with a chewy texture that works well in various recipes.

Nuts and Seeds: Nuts and seeds are nutrient-dense ingredients that offer healthy fats, protein, and a variety of vitamins and minerals. Almonds, walnuts, cashews, and peanuts are great for snacking, adding crunch to salads, or as toppings for dishes. Flaxseeds, chia seeds, hemp seeds, and sesame seeds are rich in omega-3 fatty acids and can be used in baking, smoothies, or sprinkled on top of cereals and salads.

Plant-Based Milks and Creams: Plant-based milks such as almond milk, soy milk, oat milk, and coconut milk serve as alternatives to dairy milk in cooking and baking. They add creaminess to sauces, soups, and desserts. Coconut cream and cashew cream are versatile options for creating creamy and decadent dishes.

Nutritional Yeast: Nutritional yeast is a deactivated yeast that adds a savory, cheesy flavor to dishes. It's a popular ingredient in vegan cooking, often used to make vegan cheese sauces, sprinkle on popcorn, or enhance the flavor of soups, stews, and roasted vegetables. It's a good source of B vitamins and adds depth to various recipes.

Condiments and Flavor Enhancers: Stock your pantry with a variety of condiments and flavor enhancers to add depth and complexity to your dishes. Soy sauce or tamari, balsamic vinegar, tahini, miso paste, tomato paste, Dijon mustard, and various spices and herbs are essential for creating delicious vegan meals. They provide umami, tanginess, creaminess, and aromatic notes to elevate the flavors of your dishes.

Fresh Fruits and Vegetables: Incorporating a wide variety of fresh fruits and vegetables is fundamental to vegan cooking. These ingredients provide color, texture, and a myriad of vitamins, minerals, and antioxidants. Include a rainbow of produce in your meals, such as leafy greens, bell peppers, tomatoes, onions, garlic, carrots, berries, citrus fruits, and tropical fruits, to add vibrant flavors and nutritional benefits.

Vegetable Broth and Stock: Vegetable broth or stock is a versatile ingredient that adds depth and flavor to soups, stews, and sauces. It serves as a flavorful base for many vegan recipes, providing a savory taste and enhancing the overall taste profile of your dishes. Look for low-sodium or homemade options to control the salt content.

Dried Herbs and Spices: Dried herbs and spices are essential for enhancing the flavors of your vegan dishes. Stock your spice rack with a variety of options such as basil, oregano, thyme, cumin, paprika, turmeric, cinnamon, and ginger. These aromatic additions can transform a simple meal into a flavorful delight.

Agave Nectar or Maple Syrup: Natural sweeteners like agave nectar or maple syrup are excellent alternatives to refined sugar in vegan baking and cooking. They add a touch of sweetness to desserts, dressings, sauces, and marinades. Choose high-quality, organic options for the best flavor.

Nut Butters: Nut butters such as almond butter, peanut butter, and cashew butter are versatile ingredients that can be used in both sweet and savory dishes. They add creaminess, richness, and flavor to sauces, dips, smoothies, and baked goods. Choose natural varieties without added sugars or oils.

Citrus Juices and Zest: Citrus fruits like lemons, limes, and oranges provide bright and tangy flavors to your dishes. The juice can be used in dressings, marinades, and sauces, while the zest adds a burst of aromatic flavor. They are also excellent for balancing and enhancing the taste of salads and savory dishes.

Tamari or Soy Sauce: Tamari or soy sauce adds umami and depth to vegan dishes. They are staple ingredients in stir-fries, marinades, and Asian-inspired recipes. Opt for low-sodium versions or tamari if you prefer a gluten-free option.

Canned Tomatoes and Tomato Paste: Canned tomatoes and tomato paste are pantry essentials for creating rich and flavorful sauces, soups, and stews. They provide a concentrated tomato flavor and can be used as a base for a wide range of vegan recipes. Look for varieties without added salt or sugar.

Whole Food Sweeteners: Besides agave nectar and maple syrup, other whole food sweeteners like dates, date syrup, and coconut sugar can be used to add sweetness to vegan desserts and baked goods. These natural sweeteners provide additional nutrients and are often less processed than refined sugars.

Having these essential ingredients in your kitchen will enable you to explore a wide range of flavors and create delicious vegan meals. Remember to adapt recipes to suit your preferences and experiment with different combinations to develop your own signature dishes. The possibilities in vegan cooking are endless, and with these key ingredients, you'll have the foundation to embark on a flavorful and exciting culinary journey.

Whole Grains and Legumes

Whole grains and legumes are two essential components of a healthy and balanced plant-based diet. They offer a wealth of nutrients, including fiber, protein, vitamins, and minerals, making them a valuable part of a well-rounded vegan lifestyle.

Whole grains encompass a variety of grains that retain all parts of the grain, including the bran, germ, and endosperm. This preservation of the entire grain provides a higher nutrient content and fiber compared to refined grains. Examples of whole grains include brown rice, quinoa, oats, millet, barley, and whole wheat. These grains can be cooked and used as a base for various dishes, such as grain bowls, stir-fries, soups, and salads. They offer a satisfying texture, nutty flavors, and a host of nutrients that contribute to overall health and well-being.

Legumes, on the other hand, refer to a group of plant foods that include beans, lentils, chickpeas, and peas. They are a fantastic source of plant-based protein, fiber, and carbohydrates. Legumes are incredibly versatile and can be used in a wide range of recipes. From comforting soups and stews to hearty salads, burgers, and dips, legumes provide a nutritious and filling foundation. Additionally, legumes offer an array of beneficial micronutrients like iron, folate, potassium, and magnesium, making them an important part of a vegan diet.

When whole grains and legumes are combined, they create a complementary protein profile. While legumes are rich in essential amino acids but deficient in the amino acid methionine, whole grains provide methionine but lack certain amino acids found in legumes. By consuming a combination of whole grains and legumes, such as rice and beans or lentils with quinoa, you can ensure a complete protein intake. This makes whole grains and legumes an excellent choice for vegans seeking to meet their protein needs without relying solely on animal-based sources.

Incorporating whole grains and legumes into your meals offers a multitude of health benefits. Their high fiber content supports digestive health, helps regulate blood sugar levels, and promotes a feeling of fullness, aiding in weight management. Both whole grains and legumes have been associated with a reduced risk of chronic diseases such as heart disease, type 2 diabetes, and certain cancers. Furthermore, they provide sustained energy due to their complex carbohydrates, making them an excellent choice for athletes and individuals with active lifestyles.

To incorporate whole grains and legumes into your diet, consider experimenting with different cooking methods and flavor profiles. Use whole grains as a base for grain salads, as a side dish, or as a substitute for refined grains in recipes. Legumes can be used in soups, stews, curries, salads, and even in desserts like chickpea-based cookie dough. By embracing the versatility of these plant-based powerhouses, you can create flavorful and nutritious meals that contribute to your overall well-being.

Remember to choose whole grains in their least processed form and opt for dried legumes whenever possible to minimize sodium and additives. Soaking legumes before cooking can also help reduce cooking time and enhance digestibility. With whole grains and legumes as staples in your kitchen, you'll have the foundation for countless plant-based culinary adventures while nourishing your body with the nutrients it needs to thrive.

Whole grains and legumes are integral components of a well-rounded and nourishing plant-based diet. These nutrient-rich foods offer a multitude of health benefits, including essential nutrients, dietary fiber, and plant-based proteins.

Whole grains encompass a diverse group of grains that retain their bran, germ, and endosperm, making them a superior nutritional choice compared to refined grains. Brown rice, quinoa, oats, millet, barley, and whole wheat are examples of whole grains. They are packed with fiber, vitamins, minerals, and antioxidants that contribute to overall health. Incorporating whole grains into your meals provides complex carbohydrates for sustained energy, promotes digestive health, and helps regulate blood sugar levels. With their distinct flavors and versatile cooking methods, whole grains can be enjoyed in a variety of dishes, from breakfast porridges and hearty salads to grain-based pilafs and satisfying stir-fries.

Legumes, including beans, lentils, chickpeas, and peas, are nutritional powerhouses that offer an excellent source of plant-based protein, dietary fiber, and essential micronutrients. Legumes are a cornerstone of plant-based diets, providing a wide range of health benefits. They are rich in complex carbohydrates, low in fat, and free from cholesterol. Legumes also deliver a significant amount of fiber, which promotes digestive health, aids in weight management, and helps regulate blood sugar levels. In addition, legumes offer a valuable source of plant-based protein, making them an essential component for vegans seeking to meet their protein needs. With their versatility and ability to absorb flavors, legumes can be transformed into flavorful soups, hearty stews, protein-packed salads, and delicious dips.

The combination of whole grains and legumes creates a complementary protein profile. While legumes are rich in essential amino acids but low in the amino acid methionine, whole grains provide methionine but may lack certain amino acids found in legumes. When consumed together, these two food groups complement each other and form a complete protein source, providing all the essential amino acids required by the body. This makes whole grains and legumes a valuable dietary combination for vegans and vegetarians to ensure optimal protein intake.

Incorporating whole grains and legumes into your diet not only promotes overall health but also offers environmental benefits. They are sustainable food choices, requiring fewer resources and generating fewer greenhouse gas emissions compared to animal-based protein sources. By embracing whole grains and legumes, you can contribute to a more sustainable and eco-friendly food system.

To incorporate these nutritious foods into your meals, experiment with a variety of cooking methods and flavor combinations. Prepare whole grains as a base for grain bowls, side dishes, or as a substitute for refined grains in recipes. Legumes can be cooked and used in soups, stews, curries, salads, and even incorporated into plant-based burgers or desserts. Get creative with different spices, herbs, and vegetables to enhance the flavors and create exciting culinary experiences.

With whole grains and legumes as staples in your kitchen, you have the foundation to create nourishing, satisfying, and well-balanced meals that support your health, well-being, and sustainable living. Enjoy the rich diversity of these plant-based powerhouses and embrace the abundant culinary possibilities they offer.

Whole grains and legumes are essential components of a healthy and nutritious plant-based diet. These versatile foods provide a wealth of nutrients, including fiber, protein, vitamins, and minerals, making them fundamental for maintaining overall health and well-being.

Whole grains, such as brown rice, quinoa, oats, millet, barley, and whole wheat, are grains that retain their bran, germ, and endosperm. This means they retain more of their natural fiber and nutrients compared to refined grains. Whole grains are excellent sources of complex carbohydrates, which provide sustained energy and help regulate blood sugar levels. They are also rich in dietary fiber, promoting digestive health, reducing the risk of cardiovascular diseases, and contributing to a feeling of fullness. Incorporating whole grains into your diet is as simple as cooking them and using them as a base for a variety of dishes, including grain bowls, salads, pilafs, or as a side to accompany main courses.

Legumes, including beans, lentils, chickpeas, and peas, are nutrient-dense plant foods that offer an array of health benefits. They are excellent sources of plant-based protein, fiber, complex carbohydrates, and essential micronutrients. Legumes are known for their versatility and ability to enhance the nutritional profile of meals. With their rich protein content and low-fat nature, they provide a valuable alternative to animal-based protein sources. Legumes are also high in dietary fiber, aiding in digestion, promoting a healthy gut, and helping to manage weight. Incorporating legumes into your diet is easy as they can be used in a variety of dishes such as soups, stews, curries, salads, and even in baking. They add texture, flavor, and nutritional value to your meals.

The combination of whole grains and legumes is especially powerful in a plant-based diet. Whole grains and legumes contain complementary amino acids, meaning that when consumed together, they form a complete protein source. This combination ensures that you obtain all the essential amino acids needed for optimal health. By including a variety of whole grains and legumes in your meals, you can achieve a well-balanced intake of protein and other essential nutrients necessary for proper bodily function.

Incorporating whole grains and legumes into your daily eating routine offers numerous benefits. These foods are nutrient-dense, satisfying, and contribute to overall health and well-being. They provide sustained energy, support healthy digestion, help manage weight, and reduce the risk of chronic diseases. Additionally, they are sustainable choices, requiring fewer resources and generating fewer greenhouse gas emissions compared to animal-based protein sources. By embracing whole grains and legumes, you not only nourish your body but also contribute to a more sustainable and environmentally friendly food system.

Whether you choose to enjoy a hearty lentil stew with a side of quinoa or a flavorful chickpea salad with a variety of whole grains, the combination of whole grains and legumes offers endless possibilities for creating delicious, nutritious, and satisfying plant-based meals. Get creative in the kitchen, explore different flavors and cooking techniques, and reap the many benefits of incorporating whole grains and legumes into your diet.

Plant-Based Milks and Dairy Alternatives

Plant-based milks and dairy alternatives have gained popularity as nutritious and sustainable alternatives to traditional dairy products. These plant-derived options offer a wide range of flavors, textures, and nutritional profiles, making them suitable for those following a vegan or lactose-free lifestyle, or for individuals looking to reduce their consumption of animal products.

Plant-based milks are typically made from nuts, seeds, grains, or legumes that are blended with water and strained to create a smooth and creamy beverage. Popular choices include almond milk, soy milk, oat milk, and coconut milk. These milks often come in a variety of flavors, including unsweetened, sweetened, vanilla, and chocolate, catering to different taste preferences.

Almond milk is made by blending soaked almonds with water and then straining the mixture. It has a subtle nutty flavor and a creamy consistency. Soy milk, made from soybeans, has a slightly thicker texture and a neutral taste that works well in both sweet and savory recipes. Oat milk, crafted from soaked oats blended with water, has a naturally sweet taste and a smooth texture. It is known for its versatility and ability to froth, making it a popular choice for coffee drinks. Coconut milk, made from the flesh of coconuts, has a rich and creamy texture with a distinct tropical flavor.

These plant-based milks serve as excellent substitutes for dairy milk in various applications. They can be enjoyed on their own, poured over cereal, used in smoothies, or incorporated into recipes ranging from baking to cooking. Many plant-based milks are fortified with calcium, vitamin D, and other nutrients to match or even surpass the nutritional content of dairy milk.

Dairy alternatives extend beyond plant-based milks and include a variety of products designed to mimic the taste and texture of traditional dairy items. These alternatives include plant-based yogurts, cheeses, ice creams, and butter substitutes. They are crafted using ingredients like nuts, seeds, soybeans, and coconut oil to create products that closely resemble their dairy counterparts in taste and texture.

Plant-based yogurts are typically made from soy, almond, or coconut milk and offer a creamy and tangy alternative to dairy yogurts. They come in various flavors and can be enjoyed on their own or used in recipes as a replacement for traditional yogurt. Plant-based cheeses are crafted from nuts or soybeans, offering a range of flavors and textures suitable for melting, grating, or spreading. Plant-based ice creams, made from coconut milk, almond milk, or other bases, provide a delectable frozen treat with an array of flavors and mix-ins. Butter substitutes are created using plant oils or nut-based ingredients, providing a dairy-free option for spreading on bread or using in cooking and baking.

Plant-based milks and dairy alternatives offer a variety of benefits. They are lactose-free, making them suitable for individuals with lactose intolerance. They also tend to have lower levels of saturated fats compared to dairy products. Moreover, they contribute to a more sustainable and environmentally friendly food system by reducing the demand for animal agriculture.

Plant-based milks and dairy alternatives have emerged as popular choices for individuals seeking nutritious and sustainable alternatives to traditional dairy products. These dairy-free options come in a variety of flavors, textures, and nutritional profiles, providing a range of choices for those following a vegan or lactose-free lifestyle, or simply looking to reduce their consumption of animal products.

Plant-based milks are typically made by blending nuts, seeds, grains, or legumes with water and straining the mixture to create a smooth and creamy beverage. Almond milk, soy milk, oat milk, and coconut milk are among the well-known options. Each type of milk offers its own unique flavor and texture, catering to different taste preferences.

Almond milk is created by blending soaked almonds with water and then straining the mixture, resulting in a subtly nutty flavor and a creamy consistency. Soy milk, derived from soybeans, has a slightly thicker texture and a neutral taste that makes it suitable for a variety of sweet and savory recipes. Oat milk, made from soaked oats blended with water, has a naturally sweet taste and a smooth, velvety texture. It has gained popularity for its versatility and ability to froth, making it an excellent choice for coffee drinks. Coconut milk, extracted from the flesh of coconuts, boasts a rich and creamy texture with a distinct tropical flavor.

Plant-based milks serve as excellent alternatives to dairy milk in a wide range of applications. They can be enjoyed on their own, poured over cereal, used in smoothies, or incorporated into recipes that call for milk. Many plant-based milks are fortified with calcium, vitamin D, and other nutrients to match or even surpass the nutritional content of dairy milk.

Beyond plant-based milks, dairy alternatives encompass a variety of products designed to replicate the taste and texture of traditional dairy items. These alternatives include plant-based yogurts, cheeses, ice creams, and butter substitutes. Plant-based yogurts, often made from soy, almond, or coconut milk, offer a creamy and tangy alternative to dairy yogurts, available in a range of flavors. Plant-based cheeses, crafted from nuts or soybeans, come in various styles and textures, suitable for melting, grating, or spreading. Plant-based ice creams, created from bases like coconut milk or almond milk, provide a delicious frozen treat with a multitude of flavors and mix-ins. Butter substitutes made from plant oils or nut-based ingredients offer a dairy-free option for spreading on bread or using in cooking and baking.

Opting for plant-based milks and dairy alternatives comes with a host of benefits. These products are naturally lactose-free, making them suitable for individuals with lactose intolerance. They also tend to have lower levels of saturated fats compared to traditional dairy products. Moreover, incorporating plant-based alternatives contributes to a more sustainable and environmentally friendly food system by reducing the demand for animal agriculture.

Plant-based milks and dairy alternatives have gained significant popularity as people increasingly seek nutritious and sustainable alternatives to traditional dairy products. These dairy-free options offer a wide range of flavors, textures, and nutritional profiles, making them suitable for individuals following a vegan or lactose-free lifestyle or those seeking to reduce their consumption of animal products.

Plant-based milks are typically made by blending nuts, seeds, grains, or legumes with water and then straining the mixture to create a smooth and creamy beverage. Almond milk, soy milk, oat milk, and coconut milk are among the most widely consumed plant-based milks. Each type of milk offers its own unique characteristics and taste profiles, catering to different preferences.

Almond milk is made by blending soaked almonds with water and straining the mixture, resulting in a subtly nutty flavor and a smooth, creamy texture. Soy milk, derived from soybeans, has a slightly thicker consistency and a mild taste that pairs well with both sweet and savory dishes. Oat milk, produced by blending soaked oats and water, offers a naturally sweet flavor and a rich, creamy texture. It has gained popularity for its versatility and ability to froth, making it a preferred choice for lattes and cappuccinos. Coconut milk, extracted from the flesh of coconuts, boasts a creamy and tropical flavor that adds richness to both sweet and savory recipes.

Plant-based milks serve as excellent substitutes for dairy milk in a wide range of applications. They can be enjoyed on their own, poured over cereal, used in smoothies, or incorporated into recipes that call for milk. Many plant-based milks are fortified with essential nutrients like calcium, vitamin D, and vitamin B12 to ensure they provide comparable nutritional value to dairy milk.

Dairy alternatives go beyond plant-based milks and encompass a variety of products designed to mimic the taste and texture of traditional dairy items. Plant-based yogurts, cheeses, ice creams, and butter substitutes are among the popular dairy alternatives available. Plant-based yogurts, often made from soy, almond, or coconut milk, offer a creamy and tangy alternative, available in a variety of flavors and textures. Plant-based cheeses, crafted from nuts or soybeans, provide a range of options that can be melted, grated, or spread, satisfying the craving for cheesy goodness. Plant-based ice creams, made from bases like coconut milk or almond milk, offer a delicious frozen treat with an array of flavors and mix-ins. Butter substitutes made from plant oils or nut-based ingredients provide a dairy-free option for spreading on bread or using in cooking and baking.

Choosing plant-based milks and dairy alternatives comes with several benefits. They are naturally lactose-free, making them suitable for individuals with lactose intolerance. Additionally, these alternatives often have lower levels of saturated fats compared to traditional dairy products. From an environmental standpoint, opting for plant-based alternatives helps reduce the carbon footprint associated with animal agriculture and promotes more sustainable food choices.

Incorporating plant-based milks and dairy alternatives into your diet opens up a world of diverse flavors and culinary possibilities. Whether you prefer almond milk in your morning coffee, soy yogurt in your smoothie, or coconut-based cheese on your pizza, these options provide a delicious and nutritious alternative to traditional dairy products. With an ever-expanding range of plant-based options available, you can embrace a dairy-free lifestyle while still enjoying a variety of indulgent and satisfying treats.

Natural Sweeteners and Flavor Enhancers

Natural sweeteners and flavor enhancers offer a healthier and more wholesome alternative to refined sugars and artificial additives. These natural options provide a range of tastes, textures, and aromas, enhancing the flavor profiles of various dishes while adding a touch of sweetness.

One of the most popular natural sweeteners is honey, which is produced by bees from flower nectar. Honey is known for its distinct flavor and viscosity, varying in taste depending on the types of flowers visited by the bees. It can be used in a wide array of recipes, including baked goods, dressings, and marinades. Another commonly used natural sweetener is maple syrup, derived from the sap of maple trees. It adds a rich, caramel-like flavor to dishes and is a popular choice for drizzling over pancakes, waffles, and desserts. Similarly, molasses, a byproduct of sugar production, offers a deep, robust flavor that is often used in baking and savory recipes.

Agave nectar, derived from the agave plant, is another natural sweetener that has gained popularity. It has a mild, neutral taste and a liquid consistency, making it versatile for various applications, such as sweetening beverages, desserts, and dressings. Date syrup, made from dates, offers a thick and sweet syrup with a rich flavor reminiscent of caramel. It is a great option for adding natural sweetness to baked goods and sauces.

In addition to natural sweeteners, there are various natural flavor enhancers that can elevate the taste of dishes. Vanilla extract, derived from vanilla beans, adds a warm and sweet aroma to both sweet and savory recipes. It is a staple in baking and dessert preparations. Citrus fruits, such as lemons, limes, and oranges, provide zesty and tangy flavors that brighten up salads, dressings, sauces, and desserts. Fresh herbs and spices like basil, cilantro, thyme, and cinnamon add depth and complexity to dishes, enhancing their taste and aroma.

Natural sweeteners and flavor enhancers not only provide delightful taste profiles but often come with additional nutritional benefits. For instance, honey and maple syrup contain trace amounts of minerals and antioxidants. Dates are a good source of fiber and essential minerals, while citrus fruits offer a dose of vitamin C and other beneficial compounds. By using these natural alternatives, you can enjoy the flavors you love while adding a touch of wholesome goodness to your meals and beverages.

When incorporating natural sweeteners and flavor enhancers into your recipes, it's important to consider taste balance and personal preferences. Experimenting with different combinations and quantities allows you to tailor the flavors to your liking. Remember to use them in moderation as they still contribute calories to your overall intake.

Natural sweeteners and flavor enhancers offer a healthier and more wholesome approach to adding sweetness and enhancing the taste of dishes. These natural alternatives provide a range of flavors, textures, and aromas, allowing you to elevate the flavor profiles of various recipes while reducing your reliance on refined sugars and artificial additives.

One popular natural sweetener is honey, which is produced by bees from flower nectar. Known for its distinct flavor and smooth texture, honey adds a delightful sweetness to a wide range of dishes. It can be used as a natural sweetener in baked goods, beverages, dressings, and marinades. Its taste can vary depending on the types of flowers visited by the bees, offering a diverse array of flavors to explore.

Another commonly used natural sweetener is maple syrup, derived from the sap of maple trees. With its rich, caramel-like flavor, maple syrup brings a unique and indulgent sweetness to recipes. It is a favorite choice for drizzling over pancakes, waffles, oatmeal, and desserts. Maple syrup adds depth and complexity to both sweet and savory dishes, making it a versatile and beloved ingredient.

Agave nectar is another natural sweetener gaining popularity. Derived from the agave plant, it offers a mild, neutral taste and a smooth liquid consistency. Agave nectar can be used as a substitute for sugar in a variety of recipes, such as beverages, baked goods, and dressings. Its versatility and subtle sweetness make it a popular choice for those looking for an alternative sweetener.

Date syrup, made from dates, provides a thick and sweet syrup with a rich flavor reminiscent of caramel. It is a natural sweetener that works well in baking, sauces, and dressings. Its natural sweetness adds depth and complexity to dishes, making it a great option for those seeking a natural alternative to refined sugars.

In addition to natural sweeteners, there are various natural flavor enhancers that can elevate the taste of dishes. Vanilla extract, derived from vanilla beans, adds a warm and sweet aroma to both sweet and savory recipes. It is a staple in baking and dessert preparations, imparting a delightful flavor to cakes, cookies, and custards. Citrus fruits, such as lemons, limes, and oranges, provide zesty and tangy flavors that brighten up salads, dressings, sauces, and desserts. Fresh herbs like basil, cilantro, and thyme, along with spices such as cinnamon and cumin, add depth and complexity to dishes, enhancing their taste and aroma.

Using natural sweeteners and flavor enhancers not only enhances the flavors you love but also offers additional nutritional benefits. For example, honey and maple syrup contain trace amounts of minerals and antioxidants. Dates are a good source of fiber and essential minerals, while citrus fruits provide a dose of vitamin C and other beneficial compounds. By incorporating these natural alternatives, you can enjoy the flavors you desire while adding a touch of wholesome goodness to your meals and beverages.

When using natural sweeteners and flavor enhancers, it's important to consider taste balance and personal preferences. Experimenting with different combinations and quantities allows you to customize the flavors to your liking. Remember to use them in moderation as they still contribute calories to your overall intake.

Natural sweeteners and flavor enhancers offer a healthier and more wholesome approach to adding sweetness and enhancing the taste of various dishes. These natural alternatives provide a range of flavors, textures, and aromas, allowing you to elevate the flavor profiles of your recipes while reducing your reliance on refined sugars and artificial additives.

Honey is a popular natural sweetener derived from bees' production of flower nectar. It possesses a distinct flavor and a smooth texture, making it a delightful addition to a wide range of dishes. From baked goods to beverages, dressings to marinades, honey serves as a versatile natural sweetener. The taste of honey can vary depending on the types of flowers visited by the bees, offering a diverse array of flavors to explore and enjoy.

Maple syrup, derived from the sap of maple trees, is another widely used natural sweetener. Its rich, caramel-like flavor brings a unique and indulgent sweetness to recipes. Maple syrup is beloved for its ability to enhance both sweet and savory dishes, making it a favorite choice for drizzling over pancakes, waffles, oatmeal, and desserts. Its depth and complexity make it a versatile ingredient that adds a touch of luxury to a variety of culinary creations.

Agave nectar, obtained from the agave plant, is gaining popularity as a natural sweetener. It offers a mild, neutral taste and a smooth liquid consistency, making it a great substitute for refined sugars in numerous recipes. Agave nectar can be used in beverages, baked goods, and dressings, providing a subtle sweetness that complements various flavors without overpowering them.

Date syrup, crafted from dates, offers a thick and luscious syrup with a rich caramel flavor. It serves as a natural sweetener that works exceptionally well in baking, sauces, and dressings. With its inherent sweetness, date syrup adds depth and complexity to dishes, making it a wonderful option for those seeking a natural alternative to refined sugars.

In addition to natural sweeteners, various natural flavor enhancers can elevate the taste of your dishes. Vanilla extract, derived from vanilla beans, lends a warm and sweet aroma to both sweet and savory recipes. It is a quintessential ingredient in baking and dessert preparations, imparting a delightful flavor to cakes, cookies, and custards. Citrus fruits, such as lemons, limes, and oranges, offer zesty and tangy flavors that brighten up salads, dressings, sauces, and desserts. Fresh herbs like basil, cilantro, and thyme, along with spices such as cinnamon and cumin, add depth and complexity to dishes, enhancing their taste and aroma.

Using natural sweeteners and flavor enhancers not only enhances the flavors you love but also offers additional nutritional benefits. Honey and maple syrup contain trace amounts of minerals and antioxidants, while dates are a good source of fiber and essential minerals. Citrus fruits provide a dose of vitamin C and other beneficial compounds. By incorporating these natural alternatives, you can enjoy the flavors you desire while adding a touch of wholesome goodness to your meals and beverages.

When using natural sweeteners and flavor enhancers, it's important to consider taste balance and personal preferences. Experimenting with different combinations and quantities allows you to customize the flavors to your liking. Remember to use them in moderation, as they still contribute calories to your overall intake.

By embracing natural sweeteners and flavor enhancers, you can elevate the taste of your dishes while opting for more wholesome and nutrient-rich alternatives. These natural options provide a delightful balance of flavors, adding depth and complexity to your culinary creations. With their diverse range of tastes and textures, you can enhance the enjoyment of your meals while reducing your reliance on refined sugars and artificial additives.

Chapter 4: Mastering Vegan Cooking Techniques

Cooking with Tofu and Tempeh

Cooking with tofu and tempeh opens up a world of delicious and nutritious possibilities for plant-based cooking. These versatile plant-based proteins can be transformed into a wide variety of dishes, offering unique textures and flavors that are both satisfying and satisfyingly delicious.

Tofu, made from soybean curds, is a popular choice for plant-based cooking due to its neutral taste and ability to absorb flavors. It comes in various textures, including silken, soft, firm, and extra-firm, each suitable for different cooking methods. Tofu can be marinated, grilled, sautéed, stir-fried, baked, or even blended into creamy sauces and dressings. Its soft and silky texture makes it a great addition to soups, curries, and stir-fries, while firm or extra-firm tofu can be cubed, grilled, or pan-fried for added texture and a satisfying bite. Tofu also works well as a meat substitute in dishes like tofu scramble, tofu burgers, and tofu-based desserts.

Tempeh, on the other hand, is made from fermented soybeans bound together into a firm cake. It has a nutty flavor and a dense, chewy texture that adds depth and substance to dishes. Tempeh can be marinated, sliced, grilled, pan-fried, or baked to achieve a crispy exterior while maintaining its hearty texture. It works wonderfully in sandwiches, wraps, stir-fries, and salads, adding a satisfying bite and a distinct flavor to the dish. Tempeh can also be crumbled or grated to be used as a ground meat substitute in dishes like tacos, chili, and pasta sauces.

Both tofu and tempeh are excellent sources of plant-based protein, offering essential amino acids, minerals, and vitamins. They are also low in saturated fat and cholesterol-free, making them a nutritious addition to a well-balanced diet.

When cooking with tofu and tempeh, consider marinating them beforehand to infuse them with flavor. Soy sauce, tamari, citrus juices, herbs, spices, and various sauces like barbecue or teriyaki work well as marinades. This allows the tofu or tempeh to absorb the flavors, resulting in a more flavorful end product.

Experiment with different cooking methods and flavor combinations to discover your favorite ways to enjoy tofu and tempeh. Incorporate them into stir-fries, curries, noodle dishes, salads, wraps, and even as toppings for pizzas or fillings for tacos. Tofu can also be blended into smoothies or used as a base for creamy desserts like puddings or cheesecakes.

It's important to note that tofu and tempeh can have different tastes and textures, so don't be discouraged if you don't immediately fall in love with them. Give them a few tries and explore different recipes to find your preferred cooking styles and flavors.

Cooking with tofu and tempeh opens up a world of delicious and nutritious possibilities for plant-based cooking. These versatile plant-based proteins offer unique textures and flavors that can transform your meals into satisfying and satisfyingly delicious dishes.

Tofu, made from soybean curds, is a popular choice in plant-based cooking due to its neutral taste and ability to absorb flavors. It comes in various textures, such as silken, soft, firm, and extra-firm, each suitable for different cooking methods. Tofu's versatility allows it to be marinated, grilled, sautéed, stir-fried, baked, or blended into creamy sauces and dressings. Its soft and silky texture makes it an excellent addition to soups, curries, and stir-fries, while firmer tofu varieties can be cubed, grilled, or pan-fried to provide a satisfying bite and added texture. Tofu is also a great meat substitute in dishes like tofu scramble, tofu burgers, and even tofu-based desserts.

Tempeh, on the other hand, is made from fermented soybeans bound together into a firm cake. It boasts a nutty flavor and a dense, chewy texture that adds depth and substance to dishes. Tempeh can be marinated, sliced, grilled, pan-fried, or baked to achieve a crispy exterior while maintaining its hearty texture. It lends itself well to sandwiches, wraps, stir-fries, and salads, providing a satisfying bite and a distinct flavor to the dish. Tempeh can also be crumbled or grated to serve as a ground meat substitute in dishes like tacos, chili, or pasta sauces.

Both tofu and tempeh are excellent sources of plant-based protein, offering essential amino acids, minerals, and vitamins. They are low in saturated fat and cholesterol-free, making them a nutritious addition to a well-balanced diet.

To maximize the flavor of tofu and tempeh, consider marinating them before cooking. This step infuses them with delicious flavors, enhancing their taste. Soy sauce, tamari, citrus juices, herbs, spices, and various sauces like barbecue or teriyaki work wonderfully as marinades. This allows the tofu or tempeh to soak up the flavors, resulting in a more flavorful end product.

Don't be afraid to experiment with different cooking methods and flavor combinations to discover your favorite ways to enjoy tofu and tempeh. Incorporate them into stir-fries, curries, noodle dishes, salads, wraps, and even use them as toppings for pizzas or fillings for tacos. Tofu can also be blended into smoothies or used as a base for creamy desserts like puddings or cheesecakes.

It's important to note that tofu and tempeh have their own distinct tastes and textures, so it may take a few tries to find your preferred cooking styles and flavors. Embrace the process of exploring new recipes and techniques to fully appreciate the versatility of these plant-based proteins.

Cooking with tofu and tempeh opens up a world of culinary possibilities, allowing you to create delicious and nutritious plant-based dishes. These versatile protein sources offer unique textures and flavors that can transform your meals into satisfying and flavorful creations.

Tofu, derived from soybean curds, is a staple in plant-based cooking due to its mild flavor and ability to absorb various flavors. It comes in different textures, such as silken, soft, firm, and extra-firm, each suited for different cooking methods. Tofu can be marinated, grilled, sautéed, stir-fried, baked, or blended into creamy sauces and dressings. Its soft and silky texture makes it a wonderful addition to soups, curries, and stir-fries, while firmer varieties can be cubed, grilled, or pan-fried to add a satisfying chewiness. Tofu also serves as an excellent meat substitute in dishes like tofu scrambles, tofu burgers, and even desserts.

Tempeh, made from fermented soybeans pressed into a firm cake, offers a distinct nutty flavor and a dense, chewy texture. It provides a hearty and substantial element to dishes. Tempeh can be marinated, sliced, grilled, pan-fried, or baked to achieve a crispy outer layer while maintaining its satisfyingly chewy consistency. It works wonderfully in sandwiches, wraps, stir-fries, and salads, adding a delightful bite and a unique flavor profile. Tempeh can also be crumbled or grated to serve as a ground meat substitute in dishes like tacos, chili, or pasta sauces.

Both tofu and tempeh are excellent sources of plant-based protein, offering essential amino acids, minerals, and vitamins.

They are low in saturated fat and cholesterol-free, making them a nutritious choice to support a well-rounded diet.

To enhance the flavor of tofu and tempeh, consider marinating them before cooking. This step allows the flavors to penetrate the protein, resulting in a more vibrant and satisfying taste. Soy sauce, tamari, citrus juices, herbs, spices, and various sauces like barbecue or teriyaki can be used as marinades to infuse the tofu or tempeh with delicious flavors.

Don't be afraid to experiment with different cooking methods and flavor combinations to discover your preferred ways of enjoying tofu and tempeh. Incorporate them into stir-fries, curries, noodle dishes, salads, wraps, or use them as toppings for pizzas or fillings for tacos. Tofu can also be blended into smoothies or used as a base for creamy desserts like puddings or cheesecakes.

It's important to note that tofu and tempeh have their own unique tastes and textures, which may take some time to appreciate fully. Embrace the process of exploring new recipes and techniques to unlock the full potential of these versatile plant-based proteins.

Cooking with tofu and tempeh not only adds variety to your plant-based meals but also offers a delicious way to incorporate protein into your diet. With their versatility, nutritional benefits, and ability to absorb flavors, tofu and tempeh can be transformed into delightful dishes that please your taste buds and nourish your body. So, let your culinary creativity flow, try new recipes, and savor the joys of cooking with tofu and tempeh.

Perfecting Vegan Baking

Perfecting vegan baking opens up a world of delicious possibilities, allowing you to create delectable treats without the use of animal products. While vegan baking may present some unique challenges, with a few key considerations and techniques, you can achieve exceptional results that rival traditional baked goods.

One of the primary considerations in vegan baking is finding suitable substitutes for ingredients like eggs, dairy milk, and butter. Fortunately, there are numerous options available. Flaxseed meal or chia seeds mixed with water can serve as an excellent replacement for eggs, providing binding properties and moisture. Applesauce, mashed bananas, or vegan yogurt can also act as effective egg alternatives in certain recipes, adding moisture and helping with leavening. Plant-based milk, such as almond, soy, or oat milk, can replace dairy milk in equal amounts, ensuring proper moisture and texture. For butter, coconut oil or vegan margarine can be used to achieve the desired fat content and texture.

In addition to ingredient substitutions, it's important to understand the unique characteristics of vegan ingredients. For instance, since vegan baked goods don't contain eggs, it's essential to use alternative leavening agents like baking powder or baking soda to help the batter rise. It's also helpful to include ingredients that contribute to moisture, such as fruit purees, vegetable purees, or plant-based yogurts, to ensure a tender and moist final product.

Another consideration in vegan baking is achieving the desired texture and structure. Since vegan batters tend to be denser, it's often beneficial to incorporate a combination of different flours, such as all-purpose flour, whole wheat flour, or gluten-free flour blends, to improve the texture and create a lighter result. Adding a small amount of cornstarch, arrowroot powder, or tapioca flour can also help with binding and structure.

When it comes to flavors, vegan baking offers endless possibilities. Use high-quality vanilla extract, spices like cinnamon, nutmeg, or cardamom, and other natural flavorings to enhance the taste of your creations. Don't be afraid to experiment with different ingredients like cocoa powder, citrus zest, or even vegan chocolate chips to add depth and richness to your baked goods.

Proper measuring and mixing techniques are crucial in vegan baking. Use measuring cups and spoons specifically designed for dry and wet ingredients to ensure accurate measurements. When mixing the batter, avoid overmixing, as it can lead to dense and tough textures. Instead, gently fold the ingredients together until just combined.

Finally, temperature and baking time are essential factors in vegan baking. Preheat your oven properly and monitor the baking time closely to achieve the desired texture and avoid over- or under-baking. Keep in mind that vegan baked goods may require slightly longer baking times than their non-vegan counterparts.

Perfecting vegan baking opens up a world of delicious possibilities, allowing you to create delectable treats without the use of animal products. While vegan baking may present some unique challenges, with a few key considerations and techniques, you can achieve exceptional results that rival traditional baked goods.

In vegan baking, one of the primary considerations is finding suitable substitutes for ingredients like eggs, dairy milk, and butter. Thankfully, there are numerous options available to meet your needs. Flaxseed meal or chia seeds mixed with water can serve as excellent replacements for eggs, providing the necessary binding properties and moisture. Applesauce, mashed bananas, or vegan yogurt can also act as effective egg alternatives in certain recipes, adding moisture and helping with leavening. Plant-based milk, such as almond, soy, or oat milk, can replace dairy milk in equal amounts, ensuring proper moisture and texture. For butter, coconut oil or vegan margarine can be used to achieve the desired fat content and texture in your baked goods.

In addition to ingredient substitutions, it's important to understand the unique characteristics of vegan ingredients. Without the presence of eggs, alternative leavening agents like baking powder or baking soda are used to help the batter rise. Incorporating ingredients that contribute to moisture, such as fruit purees, vegetable purees, or plant-based yogurts, is also beneficial for achieving a tender and moist final product.

Texture and structure are essential aspects of successful vegan baking. Since vegan batters tend to be denser, it's often beneficial to combine different flours, such as all-purpose flour, whole wheat flour, or gluten-free flour blends, to improve the texture and create a lighter result. Adding a small amount of cornstarch, arrowroot powder, or tapioca flour can help with binding and structure.

Flavor is another crucial element in vegan baking. Use high-quality vanilla extract, spices like cinnamon, nutmeg, or cardamom, and other natural flavorings to enhance the taste of your creations. Don't be afraid to experiment with different ingredients like cocoa powder, citrus zest, or even vegan chocolate chips to add depth and richness to your baked goods.

Proper measuring and mixing techniques are crucial in vegan baking. Use measuring cups and spoons specifically designed for dry and wet ingredients to ensure accurate measurements. When mixing the batter, avoid overmixing, as it can lead to dense and tough textures. Instead, gently fold the ingredients together until just combined.

Temperature and baking time play significant roles in vegan baking as well. Preheat your oven properly and monitor the baking time closely to achieve the desired texture and avoid over- or under-baking. Keep in mind that vegan baked goods may require slightly longer baking times than their non-vegan counterparts.

Perfecting vegan baking opens up a world of delicious possibilities, allowing you to create delectable treats without the use of animal products. While vegan baking may present some unique challenges, with a few key considerations and techniques, you can achieve exceptional results that rival traditional baked goods.

In vegan baking, one of the primary considerations is finding suitable substitutes for ingredients like eggs, dairy milk, and butter. Thankfully, there are numerous options available to meet your needs. Flaxseed meal or chia seeds mixed with water can serve as excellent replacements for eggs, providing the necessary binding properties and moisture. Applesauce, mashed bananas, or vegan yogurt can also act as effective egg alternatives in certain recipes, adding moisture and helping with leavening. Plant-based milk, such as almond, soy, or oat milk, can replace dairy milk in equal amounts, ensuring proper moisture and texture. For butter, coconut oil or vegan margarine can be used to achieve the desired fat content and texture in your baked goods.

In addition to ingredient substitutions, it's important to understand the unique characteristics of vegan ingredients. Without the presence of eggs, alternative leavening agents like baking powder or baking soda are used to help the batter rise.

Incorporating ingredients that contribute to moisture, such as fruit purees, vegetable purees, or plant-based yogurts, is also beneficial for achieving a tender and moist final product.

Texture and structure are essential aspects of successful vegan baking. Since vegan batters tend to be denser, it's often beneficial to combine different flours, such as all-purpose flour, whole wheat flour, or gluten-free flour blends, to improve the texture and create a lighter result. Adding a small amount of cornstarch, arrowroot powder, or tapioca flour can help with binding and structure.

Flavor is another crucial element in vegan baking. Use high-quality vanilla extract, spices like cinnamon, nutmeg, or cardamom, and other natural flavorings to enhance the taste of your creations. Don't be afraid to experiment with different ingredients like cocoa powder, citrus zest, or even vegan chocolate chips to add depth and richness to your baked goods.

Proper measuring and mixing techniques are crucial in vegan baking. Use measuring cups and spoons specifically designed for dry and wet ingredients to ensure accurate measurements. When mixing the batter, avoid overmixing, as it can lead to dense and tough textures. Instead, gently fold the ingredients together until just combined.

Temperature and baking time play significant roles in vegan baking as well. Preheat your oven properly and monitor the baking time closely to achieve the desired texture and avoid over- or under-baking. Keep in mind that vegan baked goods may require slightly longer baking times than their non-vegan counterparts.

With practice, patience, and a bit of experimentation, you can perfect the art of vegan baking. Embrace the learning process and enjoy the creative journey. Whether it's moist and fluffy vegan cupcakes, tender vegan cookies, or decadent vegan cakes, mastering the art of vegan baking allows you to create delightful treats that satisfy your taste buds and align with your ethical choices. So, roll up your sleeves, gather your ingredients, and let your creativity shine as you embark on the delightful adventure of perfecting vegan baking.

Sauteing, Stir-Frying, and Grilling

Sauteing, stir-frying, and grilling are versatile cooking techniques that can add depth and flavor to a wide range of ingredients. Each method offers its own unique characteristics, allowing you to create delicious and visually appealing dishes with ease.

Sauteing is a quick and straightforward cooking technique that involves cooking ingredients in a small amount of oil or fat over medium to high heat. It is ideal for cooking delicate ingredients like vegetables, tofu, or thinly sliced proteins. The high heat and relatively short cooking time help retain the natural color, texture, and flavor of the ingredients. To sauté, start by heating a small amount of oil or fat in a skillet or sauté pan. Once the oil is hot, add your ingredients and cook them quickly, stirring or tossing them frequently to ensure even cooking. The result is tender, lightly browned ingredients that retain their vibrant colors and natural flavors.

Stir-frying is a fast and high-heat cooking technique commonly associated with Asian cuisine. It involves cooking bite-sized ingredients quickly in a wok or large skillet over high heat, with constant stirring or tossing. Stir-frying allows for even cooking and imparts a distinct smoky flavor. To stir-fry, begin by heating oil in a preheated wok or skillet until it starts to smoke. Add your ingredients in stages, starting with those that take longer to cook and gradually adding the rest. Keep stirring or tossing the ingredients vigorously to prevent sticking and ensure even heat distribution. The result is a vibrant and flavorful dish with crisp and tender ingredients.

Grilling is a popular outdoor cooking method that adds a unique smoky flavor and charred texture to ingredients. It involves cooking food directly over an open flame or hot grill grates. Grilling is well-suited for a wide range of ingredients, including vegetables, tofu, tempeh, and even fruits. To grill, preheat your grill to the desired temperature. Brush the ingredients with oil or marinade to prevent sticking and enhance flavor. Place the ingredients on the grill grates and cook them until they develop grill marks and reach the desired level of doneness, flipping them as needed. The result is a deliciously charred exterior with a moist and tender interior.

When sautéing, stir-frying, or grilling, it's important to consider factors like ingredient size, cooking time, and heat control. Cut your ingredients into similar sizes to ensure even cooking. Pay attention to the cooking time and adjust the heat as needed to prevent overcooking or burning. Be mindful of the specific needs of the ingredients you're working with, as cooking times may vary.

Sautéing, stir-frying, and grilling are versatile cooking techniques that can elevate the flavors and textures of your dishes. Each method offers its own unique characteristics, allowing you to create delicious and visually appealing meals with ease.

Sautéing is a quick and simple technique that involves cooking ingredients in a small amount of oil or fat over medium to high heat. It's perfect for delicate ingredients like vegetables, tofu, or thinly sliced proteins. By using high heat and a short cooking time, sautéing helps retain the natural colors, textures, and flavors of the ingredients. To sauté, start by heating a small amount of oil or fat in a skillet or sauté pan. Once the oil is hot, add your ingredients and cook them quickly, stirring or tossing them frequently to ensure even cooking. The result is tender, lightly browned ingredients that maintain their vibrant colors and natural flavors.

Stir-frying is a fast and high-heat cooking method commonly associated with Asian cuisine. It involves cooking bite-sized ingredients quickly in a wok or large skillet over high heat, with constant stirring or tossing. Stir-frying allows for even cooking and imparts a distinct smoky flavor. To stir-fry, begin by preheating a wok or skillet and heating oil until it starts to smoke. Add your ingredients in stages, starting with those that require more cooking time and gradually adding the rest. Keep stirring or tossing the ingredients vigorously to prevent sticking and ensure even heat distribution. The result is a dish bursting with vibrant colors and flavors, with crisp and tender ingredients.

Grilling is a popular outdoor cooking technique that imparts a unique smoky flavor and charred texture to ingredients. It involves cooking food directly over an open flame or hot grill grates. Grilling works well for a wide range of ingredients, including vegetables, tofu, tempeh, and even fruits. To grill, preheat your grill to the desired temperature. Brush the ingredients with oil or marinade to prevent sticking and enhance flavor. Place the ingredients on the grill grates and cook them until they develop grill marks and reach the desired level of doneness, flipping them as needed. The result is deliciously charred exteriors with moist and tender interiors.

When sautéing, stir-frying, or grilling, it's important to consider factors like ingredient size, cooking time, and heat control. Cut your ingredients into similar sizes to ensure even cooking. Pay attention to the cooking time and adjust the heat as needed to prevent overcooking or burning. Each ingredient may have specific requirements, so be mindful of their individual needs.

These cooking techniques offer endless possibilities for creating flavorful and exciting dishes. From sautéed vegetables bursting with freshness to stir-fried noodles infused with aromatic spices, or grilled marinated tofu with a tantalizing smoky flavor, you can explore a variety of flavor combinations and culinary creations. So, whether you're sautéing, stir-frying, or grilling, let your creativity flow and embrace the art of cooking as you bring out the best in your ingredients and create delicious meals that delight both the palate and the eyes.

Sautéing, stir-frying, and grilling are versatile cooking techniques that can elevate your culinary creations, infusing them with delightful flavors and textures. Each method offers its own unique characteristics, allowing you to explore a world of delicious possibilities in the kitchen.

Sautéing is a quick and straightforward technique that involves cooking ingredients in a small amount of oil or fat over medium to high heat. It's perfect for delicate ingredients such as vegetables, tofu, or thinly sliced proteins. The high heat and short cooking time help preserve the natural colors, textures, and flavors of the ingredients. To sauté, start by heating a small amount of oil or fat in a skillet or sauté pan. Once the oil is hot, add your ingredients and cook them quickly, stirring or tossing them frequently. This ensures even cooking and prevents sticking. The result is tender, lightly browned ingredients that retain their vibrant colors and flavors.

Stir-frying, rooted in Asian cuisine, is a fast and dynamic cooking method that involves cooking bite-sized ingredients rapidly over high heat. It imparts a distinct smoky flavor and yields dishes with vibrant colors and enticing textures. To stir-fry, heat oil in a preheated wok or large skillet until it begins to smoke. Add your ingredients in stages, starting with those that require longer cooking times and gradually adding the rest. Keep the ingredients in constant motion, stirring or tossing them vigorously. This helps distribute heat evenly and ensures that each ingredient cooks quickly and evenly. The result is a dish that combines crispness and tenderness, with flavors that pop.

Grilling, a beloved outdoor cooking technique, adds a smoky flavor and appealing charred texture to ingredients. It's a versatile method suitable for vegetables, tofu, tempeh, and even fruits. Grilling brings out the natural flavors of ingredients and imparts a unique smokiness that tantalizes the taste buds. To grill, preheat your grill to the desired temperature. Brush the ingredients with oil or a flavorful marinade to prevent sticking and enhance taste. Place the ingredients directly on the grill grates and cook them until they develop beautiful grill marks and reach the desired level of doneness. Flip them as needed to ensure even cooking. The result is a dish that combines the earthy flavors of grilling with the juiciness and tenderness of the ingredients.

When sautéing, stir-frying, or grilling, it's important to consider factors like ingredient size, cooking time, and heat control. Ensure that your ingredients are cut into similar sizes to ensure uniform cooking. Adjust the heat as needed to prevent undercooking or burning. Each ingredient has its own cooking requirements, so pay attention to their specific needs.

By mastering these cooking techniques, you can create an array of flavorful and visually appealing dishes. From sautéed vegetables bursting with freshness, to stir-fried noodles infused with aromatic spices, or grilled marinated tofu with a tantalizing smoky flavor, the possibilities are endless. Embrace your creativity, experiment with different ingredients and flavors, and let sautéing, stir-frying, and grilling become the pathways to culinary excellence in your kitchen.

Steaming, Boiling, and Roasting

Steaming, boiling, and roasting are versatile cooking techniques that allow you to transform ingredients into delicious dishes with distinct flavors and textures. Each method offers its own unique characteristics, providing you with a range of options to create culinary masterpieces.

Steaming is a gentle and moist cooking technique that helps retain the natural flavors, colors, and nutrients of the ingredients. It's particularly well-suited for vegetables, seafood, and delicate proteins. To steam, start by bringing water to a boil in a pot or using a steamer basket. Place the ingredients above the boiling water, cover with a lid, and let the steam do the work. The result is tender, vibrant, and perfectly cooked food that maintains its nutritional value.

Boiling is a versatile method that involves cooking ingredients in a liquid, usually water or broth, at a rolling boil. It's ideal for pasta, grains, legumes, and hearty vegetables. To boil, bring a pot of water to a vigorous boil, add the ingredients, and cook until they reach the desired doneness. Boiling allows for even cooking and imparts flavors to the ingredients. However, be mindful of the cooking time to prevent overcooking and loss of texture or flavor.

Roasting is a dry-heat cooking method that adds depth, richness, and an irresistible aroma to a wide variety of ingredients. It's especially popular for vegetables, meats, and even fruits. To roast, preheat your oven to the desired temperature. Season the ingredients with herbs, spices, and oil, then spread them out on a baking sheet or roasting pan. Place them in the oven and let the heat work its magic, transforming the ingredients into caramelized and flavorful delights. Roasting intensifies the natural flavors, brings out sweetness, and creates a delightful contrast between the crispy exterior and tender interior.

When steaming, boiling, or roasting, it's important to consider factors like ingredient size, cooking time, and flavorings. Cut your ingredients into similar sizes to ensure even cooking. Control the cooking time to achieve the desired level of doneness and texture. Experiment with different seasonings, herbs, and spices to enhance the flavors and create unique culinary experiences.

Steaming, boiling, and roasting are versatile cooking techniques that allow you to transform ingredients into delicious dishes with distinct flavors and textures. Each method offers its own unique characteristics, providing you with a range of options to create culinary masterpieces.

Steaming is a gentle and moist cooking technique that helps retain the natural flavors, colors, and nutrients of the ingredients. It's particularly well-suited for vegetables, seafood, and delicate proteins. To steam, start by bringing water to a boil in a pot or using a steamer basket. Place the ingredients above the boiling water, cover with a lid, and let the steam envelop them. As the steam circulates, it cooks the ingredients gently and evenly. The result is tender, vibrant, and perfectly cooked food that maintains its nutritional value and natural essence.

Boiling is a versatile method that involves cooking ingredients in a liquid, usually water or broth, at a rolling boil. It's ideal for pasta, grains, legumes, and hearty vegetables. To boil, bring a pot of water or broth to a vigorous boil, add the ingredients, and cook until they reach the desired doneness. Boiling allows for even cooking and imparts flavors to the ingredients as they absorb the liquid. However, it's important to monitor the cooking time to prevent overcooking and ensure that the textures and flavors are preserved.

Roasting is a dry-heat cooking method that adds depth, richness, and an irresistible aroma to a wide variety of ingredients. It's especially popular for vegetables, meats, and even fruits. To roast, preheat your oven to the desired temperature. Season the ingredients with herbs, spices, and oil, then spread them out on a baking sheet or roasting pan. Place them in the oven and let the dry heat work its magic, transforming the ingredients into caramelized and flavorful delights. Roasting intensifies the natural flavors, brings out sweetness, and creates a delightful contrast between the crispy exterior and tender interior.

When steaming, boiling, or roasting, it's important to consider factors like ingredient size, cooking time, and flavorings. Cutting your ingredients into similar sizes ensures even cooking, while controlling the cooking time allows you to achieve the desired level of doneness and texture. Experimenting with different seasonings, herbs, and spices enhances the flavors and creates unique culinary experiences.

Steaming, boiling, and roasting are versatile cooking techniques that allow you to transform ingredients into delicious dishes with distinct flavors and textures. Each method offers its own unique characteristics, providing you with a range of options to create culinary masterpieces.

Steaming is a gentle and moist cooking technique that helps retain the natural flavors, colors, and nutrients of the ingredients. It's particularly well-suited for vegetables, seafood, and delicate proteins. To steam, start by bringing water to a boil in a pot or using a steamer basket. Place the ingredients above the boiling water, cover with a lid, and let the steam work its magic. As the steam circulates, it cooks the ingredients gently and evenly, ensuring that they remain tender and vibrant. The result is perfectly cooked food that maintains its nutritional value and natural essence.

Boiling, on the other hand, is a versatile method that involves cooking ingredients in a liquid, usually water or broth, at a rolling boil. It's ideal for pasta, grains, legumes, and hearty vegetables. To boil, bring a pot of water or broth to a vigorous boil, then add the ingredients and cook them until they reach the desired doneness. Boiling allows for even cooking and imparts flavors to the ingredients as they absorb the liquid. However, it's important to monitor the cooking time to prevent overcooking and ensure that the textures and flavors are preserved.

Roasting takes a different approach, employing dry heat to create depth, richness, and irresistible aromas. It's a popular method for vegetables, meats, and even fruits. To roast, preheat your oven to the desired temperature. Season the ingredients with herbs, spices, and oil, then place them on a baking sheet or roasting pan. The dry heat of the oven transforms the ingredients, bringing out their natural flavors and textures. Roasting creates a delightful contrast between the crispy exterior and tender interior, enhancing the overall taste and appearance of the dish.

When using these cooking techniques, it's important to consider factors such as ingredient size, cooking time, and flavorings. Cutting your ingredients into similar sizes ensures even cooking, while controlling the cooking time allows you to achieve the desired level of doneness and texture. Experimenting with different seasonings, herbs, and spices adds depth and complexity to the flavors, creating unique culinary experiences.

With steaming, boiling, and roasting in your cooking repertoire, you have the tools to create an array of delicious and visually appealing dishes. From steamed vegetables bursting with freshness and vitality, to perfectly boiled grains or pasta that are cooked to perfection, or beautifully roasted meats and vegetables that entice the senses with their enticing aromas and flavors, the possibilities are endless. So, whether you're steaming, boiling, or roasting, let your creativity flow, embrace the art of cooking, and enjoy the delightful journey of creating mouthwatering dishes that bring joy and satisfaction to your table.

Chapter 5: Special Occasions and Beyond

Vegan Entertaining and Party Foods

Vegan entertaining and party foods offer a delightful and inclusive way to host gatherings that cater to the diverse tastes and dietary preferences of your guests. Whether you're planning a casual get-together, a festive celebration, or a themed party, there are endless possibilities for creating delicious vegan dishes that will leave everyone impressed and satisfied.

When it comes to vegan entertaining, it's important to consider a balance of flavors, textures, and presentation. Start by crafting a menu that features a variety of appetizers, main courses, sides, and desserts, ensuring there is something for everyone to enjoy. Focus on using fresh, seasonal ingredients to create vibrant and visually appealing dishes that showcase the beauty of plant-based cuisine.

For appetizers, think beyond the traditional cheese and meat platters. Consider assembling colorful vegetable crudités with a selection of flavorful dips like hummus, guacamole, or dairy-free ranch dressing. Bite-sized vegan sushi rolls, crispy spring rolls, or stuffed mushroom caps are also crowd-pleasers. These options offer a range of flavors and textures, enticing guests to explore the diverse world of vegan appetizers.

When it comes to main courses, explore plant-based options that are hearty and satisfying. Consider dishes like stuffed bell peppers, vegetable stir-fries with tofu or tempeh, flavorful plant-based burgers or sliders, or even vegan lasagna or enchiladas. These dishes can be packed with savory flavors, aromatic spices, and a variety of vegetables, providing a substantial and satisfying meal for your guests.

Sides are an essential part of any meal, and vegan options can be just as delicious and varied. Consider roasted vegetables, quinoa or couscous salads, flavorful grain bowls, or even creamy mashed potatoes made with dairy-free alternatives. These sides can add depth and variety to the meal, complementing the main dishes and ensuring a well-rounded dining experience.

Desserts are a sweet finale to any gathering. Indulge your guests with an array of vegan treats such as fruit tarts, vegan chocolate mousse, plant-based cheesecakes, or delectable vegan cookies and brownies. These desserts can be made with ingredients like plant-based milks, coconut cream, and natural sweeteners, creating rich and satisfying flavors that will impress even the most discerning sweet tooth.

Vegan entertaining and party foods provide a delightful and inclusive way to host gatherings that cater to the diverse tastes and dietary preferences of your guests. Whether you're planning a casual get-together, a festive celebration, or a themed party, there are endless possibilities for creating delicious vegan dishes that will leave everyone impressed and satisfied.

When it comes to vegan entertaining, it's important to consider a balance of flavors, textures, and presentation. Craft a menu that features a variety of appetizers, main courses, sides, and desserts, ensuring there is something for everyone to enjoy. Focus on using fresh, seasonal ingredients to create vibrant and visually appealing dishes that showcase the beauty of plant-based cuisine.

For appetizers, think beyond the traditional cheese and meat platters. Create an enticing spread of colorful vegetable crudités paired with flavorful dips like hummus, guacamole, or dairy-free ranch dressing. Serve bite-sized vegan sushi rolls filled with vibrant vegetables or crispy spring rolls bursting with savory fillings. Stuffed mushroom caps filled with seasoned breadcrumbs or herbed tofu can also be a hit. These options offer a range of flavors and textures, enticing guests to explore the diverse world of vegan appetizers.

When it comes to main courses, explore plant-based options that are hearty and satisfying. Consider dishes like stuffed bell peppers filled with quinoa and vegetables, vegetable stir-fries with marinated tofu or tempeh, flavorful plant-based burgers or sliders loaded with toppings, or even comforting vegan lasagna or enchiladas filled with layers of vegetables and vegan cheese. These dishes can be packed with savory flavors, aromatic spices, and a variety of vegetables, providing a substantial and satisfying meal for your guests.

Sides are an essential part of any meal, and vegan options can be just as delicious and varied. Consider roasted vegetables seasoned with herbs and spices, vibrant quinoa or couscous salads bursting with fresh ingredients, flavorful grain bowls with a variety of toppings and dressings, or even creamy mashed potatoes made with dairy-free alternatives. These sides can add depth and variety to the meal, complementing the main dishes and ensuring a well-rounded dining experience.

Desserts are a sweet finale to any gathering, and vegan options are no exception. Indulge your guests with an array of vegan treats such as fruit tarts with a buttery vegan crust, velvety vegan chocolate mousse made with rich plant-based chocolate, plant-based cheesecakes with nutty crusts and creamy fillings, or delectable vegan cookies and brownies packed with chocolate chips or nuts. These desserts can be made with ingredients like plant-based milks, coconut cream, and natural sweeteners, creating rich and satisfying flavors that will impress even the most discerning sweet tooth.

Vegan entertaining and party foods offer a delightful and inclusive way to host gatherings that cater to the diverse tastes and dietary preferences of your guests. Whether you're planning a casual get-together, a festive celebration, or a themed party, there are endless possibilities for creating delicious vegan dishes that will leave everyone impressed and satisfied.

When it comes to vegan entertaining, it's important to consider a balance of flavors, textures, and presentation. Craft a menu that features a variety of appetizers, main courses, sides, and desserts, ensuring there is something for everyone to enjoy. Focus on using fresh, seasonal ingredients to create vibrant and visually appealing dishes that showcase the beauty of plant-based cuisine.

For appetizers, think beyond the traditional cheese and meat platters. Create an enticing spread of colorful vegetable crudités paired with flavorful dips like hummus, guacamole, or dairy-free ranch dressing. Serve bite-sized vegan sushi rolls filled with vibrant vegetables or crispy spring rolls bursting with savory fillings. Stuffed mushroom caps filled with seasoned breadcrumbs or herbed tofu can also be a hit. These options offer a range of flavors and textures, enticing guests to explore the diverse world of vegan appetizers.

When it comes to main courses, explore plant-based options that are hearty and satisfying. Consider dishes like stuffed bell peppers filled with quinoa and vegetables, vegetable stir-fries with marinated tofu or tempeh, flavorful plant-based burgers or sliders loaded with toppings, or even comforting vegan lasagna or enchiladas filled with layers of vegetables and vegan cheese. These dishes can be packed with savory flavors, aromatic spices, and a variety of vegetables, providing a substantial and satisfying meal for your guests.

Sides are an essential part of any meal, and vegan options can be just as delicious and varied. Consider roasted vegetables seasoned with herbs and spices, vibrant quinoa or couscous salads bursting with fresh ingredients, flavorful grain bowls with a variety of toppings and dressings, or even creamy mashed potatoes made with dairy-free alternatives. These sides can add depth and variety to the meal, complementing the main dishes and ensuring a well-rounded dining experience.

Desserts are a sweet finale to any gathering, and vegan options are no exception. Indulge your guests with an array of vegan treats such as fruit tarts with a buttery vegan crust, velvety vegan chocolate mousse made with rich plant-based chocolate, plant-based cheesecakes with nutty crusts and creamy fillings, or delectable vegan cookies and brownies packed with chocolate chips or nuts. These desserts can be made with ingredients like plant-based milks, coconut cream, and natural sweeteners, creating rich and satisfying flavors that will impress even the most discerning sweet tooth.

To elevate the experience further, consider incorporating thematic elements into your vegan entertaining. Whether it's a Mexican fiesta with vibrant salsas, fresh guacamole, and flavorful tacos, an Asian-inspired feast with stir-fried noodles, vegetable spring rolls, and tangy sauces, or a Mediterranean-themed soirée featuring colorful mezze platters, stuffed grape leaves, and aromatic herbs, infusing your menu with complementary flavors, spices, and dishes will add an extra layer of excitement to the gathering.

With vegan entertaining and party foods, you can showcase the versatility and creativity of plant-based cuisine while ensuring that all your guests are treated to a memorable and enjoyable dining experience. So, get inspired, explore new flavors and ingredients, and let your creativity shine as you host gatherings that celebrate delicious vegan food and the joy of sharing it with others.

Hosting a Vegan Dinner Party

Hosting a vegan dinner party is a wonderful way to showcase the delicious flavors and variety of plant-based cuisine while providing a memorable and enjoyable experience for your guests. Whether your guests are vegan, vegetarian, or simply open to trying new culinary delights, a vegan dinner party can impress and inspire with its creative and flavorful dishes. Here are some tips to help you plan and execute a successful vegan dinner party:

Menu Planning: Start by planning a well-balanced menu that incorporates a variety of flavors, textures, and colors. Consider dishes from different cuisines to offer a diverse dining experience. Include appetizers, main courses, sides, and desserts, ensuring there are options to suit different tastes and dietary needs.

Ingredient Selection: Choose fresh, seasonal, and high-quality ingredients to maximize the flavors of your dishes. Incorporate a variety of vegetables, legumes, whole grains, nuts, and seeds to create a balanced and satisfying meal.

Appetizers and Starters: Offer a selection of flavorful appetizers to kick off the evening. This can include a vibrant salad with mixed greens and colorful vegetables, a platter of marinated olives and roasted nuts, or a refreshing gazpacho soup. These options will whet your guests' appetites while showcasing the versatility of vegan ingredients.

Main Course Brilliance: Create impressive main courses that are both visually appealing and delicious. Consider dishes like stuffed bell peppers with quinoa and vegetable filling, mushroom Wellington with a flaky crust, or a flavorful curry with tofu and seasonal vegetables. These options will highlight the richness and variety of plant-based cuisine.

Sides and Accompaniments: Complement your main courses with flavorful and diverse side dishes. Serve roasted vegetables with herbs and spices, a colorful grain salad with roasted chickpeas, or a creamy vegan mashed potato. These sides will add depth and variety to the meal.

Desserts to Delight: End the evening on a sweet note with delectable vegan desserts. Consider options like a luscious vegan chocolate cake, a refreshing fruit sorbet, or a creamy coconut-based pudding. These desserts will satisfy any sweet tooth while demonstrating the indulgent possibilities of vegan treats.

Beverage Selection: Choose a variety of vegan-friendly beverages to accompany the meal. Offer a selection of wines, craft beers, or signature vegan cocktails. Also, consider providing non-alcoholic options like infused water, herbal teas, or refreshing mocktails.

Communication: Clearly communicate to your guests that the dinner party is vegan-themed, so they can come prepared and embrace the experience. If they have any specific dietary requirements or allergies, be sure to accommodate their needs by providing suitable options.

Table Setting and Ambience: Create an inviting and beautiful table setting to enhance the dining experience. Use vibrant table linens, elegant dinnerware, and fresh flowers or greenery as centerpieces. Set the mood with soft lighting and soothing background music.

Enjoy the Experience: As the host, relax and enjoy the party along with your guests. Share the stories behind the dishes and engage in conversations about veganism and its benefits. Encourage your guests to appreciate the flavors and textures of the food, and let them experience the joy of a vegan meal.

Interactive Elements: Incorporate interactive elements to engage your guests and make the dinner party even more enjoyable. Consider setting up a DIY taco or sushi bar where guests can assemble their own creations using a variety of vegan fillings and toppings. This adds a fun and interactive element to the meal, allowing everyone to personalize their dishes.

Vegan Cheese and Charcuterie Board: Create a vegan cheese and charcuterie board as a centerpiece for your appetizer spread. Include an assortment of vegan cheeses made from nuts or plant-based ingredients, along with a selection of vegan deli slices, pickles, olives, and crusty bread. This provides a visually appealing and delicious option for guests to enjoy.

Seasonal and Local Ingredients: Emphasize the use of seasonal and locally sourced ingredients in your dishes. Not only does this support local farmers and promote sustainability, but it also ensures that your ingredients are at their peak freshness and flavor. Consider visiting a farmers market to discover unique and fresh produce for your menu.

Creative Vegan Cocktails: Serve creative and refreshing vegan cocktails to complement the flavors of your dishes. Experiment with fruit-infused spritzers, herb-based mocktails, or signature vegan cocktails made with plant-based spirits. Provide recipe cards for guests to recreate their favorite drinks at home.

Vegan Cheese and Dessert Tastings: Arrange a vegan cheese or dessert tasting experience where guests can sample a variety of plant-based cheeses or decadent desserts. Provide tasting notes and pairings to enhance the experience and encourage discussion among guests about their favorites.

Cooking Demonstrations: Consider incorporating cooking demonstrations into your dinner party. Show guests how to prepare a simple vegan dish or share tips and techniques for plant-based cooking. This interactive element can spark conversations, inspire guests to try new recipes, and deepen their appreciation for vegan cuisine.

Thoughtful Accommodations: In addition to providing vegan options, consider accommodating other dietary restrictions or preferences of your guests. Offer gluten-free or nut-free alternatives for those with specific allergies or sensitivities. This demonstrates your attentiveness and ensures that everyone can enjoy the meal without any concerns.

Sustainable Tableware: Opt for eco-friendly and sustainable tableware options, such as compostable plates, cups, and utensils made from plant-based materials. This reduces the environmental impact of your dinner party and aligns with the values of veganism and sustainability.

Party Favors: Send your guests home with thoughtful party favors that align with the theme of the evening. Consider small packages of homemade vegan cookies, recipe cards, or eco-friendly gifts like reusable tote bags or stainless steel straws. This serves as a token of appreciation and leaves a lasting impression on your guests.

Post-Dinner Discussion: After the meal, initiate a discussion or Q&A session about veganism, plant-based diets, or sustainability. Encourage guests to share their thoughts, experiences, and any questions they may have. This promotes a deeper understanding of veganism and encourages dialogue among guests.

By incorporating these additional tips, you can elevate your vegan dinner party to an extraordinary and unforgettable event. Create an atmosphere of enjoyment, foster connections among guests, and inspire them to explore the world of vegan cuisine beyond the dinner party itself.

Elegant Appetizers and Finger Foods

Elegant appetizers and finger foods are the perfect way to kick off any gathering with style and sophistication. These delectable bite-sized creations are not only visually appealing but also bursting with flavors and textures that will delight your guests' palates. Whether you're hosting a formal dinner party, a cocktail soirée, or a special occasion, incorporating elegant appetizers and finger foods adds a touch of elegance to your event.

When it comes to creating elegant appetizers and finger foods, presentation is key. Start by selecting high-quality ingredients that are fresh, seasonal, and flavorful. Aim for a balance of colors, shapes, and textures to create visually stunning platters that will entice your guests from the moment they arrive.

One option for elegant appetizers is to assemble elegant bruschetta. Toasted baguette slices can serve as a base, topped with a variety of creative and delicious combinations. Consider traditional toppings like fresh tomatoes, basil, and garlic-infused olive oil, or explore unique flavor profiles such as roasted red peppers with vegan cream cheese and balsamic reduction, or caramelized onions with fig jam and vegan blue cheese crumbles.

These bruschetta variations offer a harmonious blend of flavors and textures that will impress your guests.

Another elegant option is to create sophisticated and artistic skewers. Skewers allow for endless possibilities, combining different ingredients into visually striking arrangements. For example, create colorful caprese skewers with cherry tomatoes, basil leaves, and vegan mozzarella balls, drizzled with balsamic glaze. Alternatively, assemble Mediterranean-inspired skewers with marinated artichoke hearts, olives, and grilled zucchini. These bite-sized delights are not only visually appealing but also packed with layers of complementary flavors.

For a touch of elegance and refinement, consider serving stuffed mushrooms. Choose large, firm mushrooms and stuff them with flavorful fillings such as vegan cream cheese, spinach, and garlic, or a mixture of quinoa, roasted vegetables, and herbs. The mushrooms can be baked until tender and golden, resulting in savory bites that are as pleasing to the eye as they are to the taste buds.

Elegant appetizers and finger foods can also include delicate and artistic sushi rolls. Create visually stunning rolls with colorful vegetables, avocado, and marinated tofu, wrapped in nori seaweed and served with soy sauce, pickled ginger, and wasabi. The combination of fresh ingredients, precise rolling techniques, and beautiful plating will make these sushi rolls a standout addition to your elegant spread.

To complete your selection of elegant appetizers and finger foods, don't forget to include a variety of dips, spreads, and artisanal crackers or breadsticks. Offer options like creamy hummus with toasted pine nuts, roasted red pepper dip with pita triangles, or vegan cheese spreads with an assortment of gourmet crackers. These accompaniments add depth and variety to your appetizer spread while providing additional opportunities for guests to indulge in delicious flavors.

When serving elegant appetizers and finger foods, pay attention to details such as garnishes, drizzles, and artistic plating. Fresh herbs, edible flowers, or a drizzle of infused oils can elevate the presentation and add a touch of sophistication to each dish.

Elegant appetizers and finger foods are the perfect way to elevate any gathering and add a touch of sophistication to your event. These bite-sized creations not only tantalize the taste buds but also dazzle the eyes with their beautiful presentation. Whether you're hosting a formal dinner party, a cocktail soirée, or a special occasion, incorporating elegant appetizers and finger foods will impress your guests and set the stage for an unforgettable culinary experience.

When crafting elegant appetizers and finger foods, attention to detail and creativity are key. Begin by selecting high-quality ingredients that are fresh, seasonal, and bursting with flavor. Aim to create a harmonious balance of colors, shapes, and textures to create visually stunning platters that will entice your guests from the moment they arrive.

One exquisite option for elegant appetizers is the art of bruschetta. Toasted baguette slices serve as the perfect canvas for a variety of flavorful combinations. Consider traditional toppings like vine-ripened tomatoes, fragrant basil leaves, and a drizzle of garlic-infused olive oil. Or, venture into more inventive territory with roasted red peppers, velvety vegan cream cheese, and a tangy balsamic reduction. These bruschetta variations offer a delightful medley of flavors and textures that will impress even the most discerning palates.

Another elegant choice is to create sophisticated and visually striking skewers. Skewers allow for endless possibilities, allowing you to combine ingredients in artistic arrangements. For example, assemble vibrant caprese skewers with plump cherry tomatoes, fragrant basil leaves, and luscious vegan mozzarella balls, all delicately drizzled with a reduction of balsamic glaze. Alternatively, create Mediterranean-inspired skewers featuring marinated artichoke hearts, briny olives, and perfectly grilled zucchini. These bite-sized delights not only showcase an array of flavors but also serve as stunning edible works of art.

For an added touch of refinement, consider serving stuffed mushrooms. Select large, firm mushrooms and fill them with delectable combinations such as vegan cream cheese blended with wilted spinach and fragrant garlic. Alternatively, stuff them with a savory mixture of quinoa, roasted vegetables, and aromatic herbs. Baked until tender and golden, these stuffed mushrooms offer an elegant and flavorful treat that is sure to impress your guests.

Elegant appetizers and finger foods can also include delicate and artfully prepared sushi rolls. Craft visually stunning rolls filled with a vibrant array of vegetables, creamy avocado, and marinated tofu, all delicately wrapped in nori seaweed. Serve them alongside soy sauce, pickled ginger, and wasabi for an authentic touch. The combination of fresh ingredients, precise rolling techniques, and beautiful plating will make these sushi rolls a standout addition to your elegant spread.

To complete your selection of elegant appetizers and finger foods, don't forget to include a variety of dips, spreads, and artisanal crackers or breadsticks. Offer options like velvety hummus adorned with toasted pine nuts, a smoky roasted red pepper dip paired with crispy pita triangles, or a selection of vegan cheese spreads accompanied by an assortment of gourmet crackers. These accompaniments add depth and variety to your appetizer spread while providing additional opportunities for guests to indulge in a delightful array of flavors.

Remember to pay attention to the finishing touches when serving elegant appetizers and finger foods. A sprinkle of fresh herbs, a delicate edible flower, or a drizzle of infused oil can transform each dish into a work of culinary art, enhancing both the visual appeal and the flavor profile.

Elegant appetizers and finger foods are a delightful way to elevate any gathering, offering a sophisticated and enticing culinary experience for your guests. These bite-sized creations not only excite the taste buds but also captivate the eyes with their impeccable presentation. Whether you're hosting a formal dinner party, a cocktail soirée, or a special occasion, incorporating elegant appetizers and finger foods adds a touch of refinement and indulgence to your event.

When crafting elegant appetizers and finger foods, attention to detail and creativity are essential. Begin by selecting high-quality ingredients that are fresh, seasonal, and bursting with flavor. The key is to create a harmonious balance of colors, shapes, and textures to design visually stunning platters that will captivate your guests from the moment they arrive.

One exquisite option for elegant appetizers is the art of bruschetta. Crispy baguette slices serve as the perfect canvas for a variety of flavor combinations. Opt for traditional toppings like juicy vine-ripened tomatoes, aromatic basil leaves, and a drizzle of garlic-infused olive oil for a classic and refreshing bite. Alternatively, explore more adventurous variations such as tangy sun-dried tomatoes with creamy vegan feta and a sprinkle of fresh herbs. These bruschetta variations offer a delightful medley of flavors and textures that will leave your guests longing for more.

Another elegant choice is to create visually stunning skewers. Skewers provide a canvas for your culinary artistry, allowing you to combine ingredients in visually striking arrangements. Consider assembling colorful caprese skewers with vibrant cherry tomatoes, fragrant basil leaves, and delectable vegan mozzarella pearls, all elegantly drizzled with a tangy balsamic reduction. For a touch of Mediterranean sophistication, skewer marinated artichoke hearts, briny olives, and succulent grilled eggplant, creating a tantalizing taste of the Mediterranean on a stick. These bite-sized delights not only offer a symphony of flavors but also serve as captivating edible works of art.

For an added touch of refinement, turn to stuffed mushrooms. Choose plump and hearty mushrooms and fill them with delectable fillings such as creamy vegan cheese mixed with earthy herbs or a savory mixture of quinoa, roasted vegetables, and aromatic spices. Baked to perfection, these stuffed mushrooms offer a burst of flavor in an elegant and convenient package, making them a crowd-pleasing addition to your appetizer spread.

Elegant appetizers and finger foods can also include delicate and artfully prepared sushi rolls. Craft visually stunning rolls with vibrant vegetables, creamy avocado, and delicate strips of marinated tofu, all meticulously wrapped in nori seaweed. Serve them alongside soy sauce, pickled ginger, and wasabi for a touch of authenticity. The combination of fresh ingredients, precise rolling techniques, and beautiful plating will make these sushi rolls a standout addition to your elegant spread.

To complete your selection of elegant appetizers and finger foods, don't forget to include a variety of dips, spreads, and artisanal crackers or breadsticks. Offer options like velvety hummus adorned with a drizzle of fragrant extra virgin olive oil, a smoky roasted red pepper dip served with crispy pita triangles, or a selection of vegan cheese spreads paired with delicate artisanal crackers. These accompaniments add depth and variety to your appetizer spread while providing guests with a delightful range of flavors and textures.

By incorporating elegant appetizers and finger foods into your event, you set the tone for a memorable and refined dining experience. These bite-sized creations not only impress with their beautiful presentation but also captivate guests with their harmonious flavors and textures. So, let your creativity soar, embrace the art of presentation, and create a captivating array of elegant appetizers and finger foods that will leave your guests in awe.

Refreshing Mocktails and Party Drinks

Refreshing mocktails and party drinks are a delightful way to quench guests' thirst and add a touch of vibrancy to any gathering. These alcohol-free concoctions offer a wide array of flavors, colors, and textures that will captivate your guests' taste buds and create a festive atmosphere. Whether you're hosting a summer barbecue, a birthday celebration, or a casual get-together, incorporating refreshing mocktails and party drinks ensures that everyone can partake in the festivities and enjoy delicious beverages that are as visually appealing as they are flavorful.

When it comes to crafting refreshing mocktails and party drinks, creativity and attention to detail are key. Begin by selecting a variety of fresh fruits, herbs, and other flavorings that will serve as the foundation for your drinks. Opt for seasonal ingredients to maximize the flavors and add a touch of seasonal flair to your beverage menu.

One popular option for refreshing mocktails is the classic virgin mojito. Muddle together fresh mint leaves, lime wedges, and a touch of sugar or simple syrup in a glass. Add a splash of sparkling water or soda water and plenty of ice, then garnish with a sprig of mint and a lime wheel. The result is a zesty, mint-infused drink that is both refreshing and invigorating.

For a tropical twist, consider a virgin piña colada. Blend together fresh pineapple chunks, coconut milk or coconut water, and a handful of ice until smooth and creamy. Pour into a chilled glass, garnish with a pineapple wedge or a cherry, and serve with a colorful straw. The creamy texture and tropical flavors make this mocktail a crowd favorite.

Another option is to create a vibrant and refreshing fruit punch. Combine a variety of freshly squeezed fruit juices such as orange, pineapple, and cranberry in a large pitcher. Add a splash of lemon or lime juice for a tangy kick, and sweeten with a touch of agave syrup or maple syrup. Stir well, then serve over ice with a garnish of fresh fruit slices. This fruit punch is not only visually stunning but also bursting with fruity flavors that will quench your guests' thirst.

To add an elegant touch, consider serving a sparkling mocktail. Combine a splash of freshly squeezed citrus juice, such as grapefruit or blood orange, with a flavored syrup like elderflower or raspberry. Top it off with chilled sparkling water or sparkling apple cider, and garnish with a twist of citrus peel or a fresh berry. The effervescence and delicate flavors make this mocktail a sophisticated and refreshing choice.

For a non-alcoholic twist on a classic cocktail, create a virgin mule. Combine ginger beer or ginger ale with freshly squeezed lime juice and a dash of aromatic bitters. Serve over ice in a copper mug and garnish with a lime wedge and a sprig of fresh mint. The zingy flavors of ginger and lime create a refreshing and invigorating mocktail that is sure to impress.

When serving refreshing mocktails and party drinks, consider using decorative glassware, colorful straws, and fresh garnishes to enhance the presentation. Allow guests to customize their mocktails with a selection of fresh fruits, herbs, and flavored syrups for a personalized touch.

Refreshing mocktails and party drinks are the perfect way to add a burst of flavor and a touch of celebration to any gathering. These alcohol-free concoctions are crafted with a variety of ingredients, from fresh fruits and herbs to flavorful syrups and sparkling beverages, creating delightful and invigorating beverages that can be enjoyed by guests of all ages. Whether you're hosting a summer garden party, a festive holiday gathering, or a casual get-together, incorporating refreshing mocktails and party drinks ensures that everyone can savor delicious and visually stunning beverages that are as refreshing as they are appealing.

When it comes to crafting refreshing mocktails and party drinks, let your imagination run wild. Start by selecting a range of fresh and seasonal ingredients that will serve as the foundation for your creations. This could include juicy citrus fruits, ripe berries, fragrant herbs like mint or basil, or even exotic flavors like coconut or passion fruit.

One classic option for a refreshing mocktail is the virgin mojito. In a tall glass, muddle together fresh mint leaves, lime wedges, and a touch of sugar or simple syrup until the mint releases its aromatic oils. Add plenty of ice and top it off with sparkling water or soda water for a fizzy kick. Garnish with a sprig of fresh mint and a lime wheel for an elegant touch. The combination of tangy lime, invigorating mint, and effervescent bubbles creates a refreshing and uplifting beverage.

For a taste of the tropics, consider a virgin piña colada. In a blender, blend together fresh pineapple chunks, creamy coconut milk or coconut water, and a handful of ice until smooth and creamy. Pour the mixture into a chilled glass, garnish with a pineapple wedge or a maraschino cherry, and serve with a colorful straw. The tropical flavors and creamy texture transport your guests to a sunny paradise, making it a perfect choice for warm-weather gatherings.

If you're looking for a vibrant and fruity option, a fruit punch is a fantastic choice. Combine a variety of freshly squeezed fruit juices, such as orange, pineapple, and cranberry, in a large pitcher. Add a splash of lemon or lime juice for a tangy twist and sweeten with a touch of agave syrup or honey. Stir well to combine all the flavors, then serve the punch over ice with a garnish of fresh fruit slices. The combination of different fruit flavors creates a refreshing and thirst-quenching beverage that is visually appealing and bursting with fruity goodness.

To add a touch of elegance and effervescence to your gathering, serve sparkling mocktails. Combine a splash of freshly squeezed citrus juice, such as grapefruit or blood orange, with a flavored syrup like elderflower or raspberry. Top it off with chilled sparkling water or sparkling apple cider for a delightful fizz.

Garnish the glass with a twist of citrus peel or a fresh berry to enhance the presentation. The sparkling bubbles and delicate flavors create a sophisticated and refreshing mocktail that is sure to impress your guests.

For those who enjoy the flavors of classic cocktails, a virgin mule is a fantastic choice. Combine ginger beer or ginger ale with freshly squeezed lime juice and a dash of aromatic bitters. Serve the mocktail over ice in a copper mug for an authentic touch, and garnish with a lime wedge and a sprig of fresh mint. The combination of zingy ginger, tangy lime, and cooling mint creates a refreshing and invigorating beverage that is perfect for any occasion.

Refreshing mocktails and party drinks are the ultimate way to quench your guests' thirst and infuse your gathering with a burst of flavor and excitement. These alcohol-free beverages are carefully crafted using a variety of ingredients, from fresh fruits and herbs to flavorful syrups and sparkling elements, resulting in delightful and invigorating drinks that can be enjoyed by all. Whether you're hosting a summer pool party, a festive holiday gathering, or a casual get-together, incorporating refreshing mocktails and party drinks ensures that everyone can revel in delicious and visually captivating beverages that are as refreshing as they are enticing.

When it comes to concocting refreshing mocktails and party drinks, the possibilities are endless. Begin by selecting a range of fresh, seasonal ingredients that will serve as the foundation for your creations. Think juicy citrus fruits, succulent berries, aromatic herbs like mint or basil, or even exotic flavors like coconut or passion fruit.

One classic option for a refreshing mocktail is the iconic virgin mojito. In a tall glass, muddle together a handful of fresh mint leaves, lime wedges, and a touch of sugar or simple syrup until the mint releases its invigorating aroma. Fill the glass with plenty of ice and top it off with sparkling water or soda water to lend a sparkling effervescence. Garnish with a sprig of fresh mint and a lime wheel for an elegant touch. The combination of tangy lime, refreshing mint, and lively bubbles creates a truly revitalizing and uplifting beverage.

For a taste of the tropics, a virgin piña colada is an excellent choice. Blend together chunks of fresh pineapple, creamy coconut milk or coconut water, and a generous amount of ice until the mixture turns smooth and luscious. Pour this tropical blend into a chilled glass, garnish with a pineapple wedge or a vibrant maraschino cherry, and serve with a colorful straw. The tropical flavors and velvety texture transport your guests to a sun-drenched paradise, making it an ideal option for warm-weather celebrations.

If you're looking to serve a vibrant and fruity delight, a fruit punch will never disappoint. In a large pitcher, combine an assortment of freshly squeezed fruit juices such as orange, pineapple, and cranberry. Add a splash of zesty lemon or lime juice for a tangy twist, and sweeten the concoction with a touch of agave syrup or honey. Stir well to blend all the flavors harmoniously, then serve the punch over ice, garnishing with slices of fresh fruit to add an inviting touch. The medley of different fruit flavors creates a refreshing and thirst-quenching beverage that is visually captivating and brimming with fruity goodness.

To infuse your gathering with elegance and effervescence, sparkling mocktails are a superb choice. Combine a splash of freshly squeezed citrus juice—grapefruit or blood orange, for instance—with a flavored syrup like elderflower or raspberry. Crown the mixture with chilled sparkling water or sparkling apple cider to introduce a delightful effervescence. Enhance the presentation with a twist of citrus peel or a plump fresh berry. The sparkling bubbles and delicate flavors meld together to create a sophisticated and refreshing mocktail that will impress your guests.

For those who enjoy the flavors of classic cocktails without the alcohol, a virgin mule is an exceptional option. Combine ginger beer or ginger ale with a generous squeeze of lime juice and a dash of aromatic bitters. Serve this invigorating mocktail over ice in a classic copper mug, garnishing with a lime wedge and a sprig of fresh mint for a touch of elegance. The marriage of zesty ginger, tangy lime, and cooling mint generates a refreshing and revitalizing beverage.

By incorporating refreshing mocktails and party drinks into your gathering, you provide a delightful and inclusive beverage experience for all your guests. These flavorful concoctions not only quench thirst but also add a touch of elegance and vibrancy to your event. So, let your creativity flow, experiment with different flavor combinations, and create a beverage menu that will leave your guests refreshed and delighted throughout the celebration.

Chapter 6: Vegan on the Go: Quick and Easy Meals

Portable Lunch Ideas

Portable lunch ideas are a game-changer for those who are constantly on the go or prefer to enjoy their meals outside of the traditional dining setting. These convenient and delicious meals are designed to be easily packed and carried, allowing you to enjoy a satisfying lunch wherever your day takes you. Whether you're headed to work, school, a picnic, or simply out and about, incorporating portable lunch ideas ensures that you can savor a nutritious and flavorful meal without compromising on taste or convenience.

When it comes to crafting portable lunches, versatility and practicality are key. Start by selecting ingredients that are both delicious and capable of withstanding transportation. Opt for sturdy containers that are leak-proof and well-sealed to keep your meal fresh and intact. Consider using compartmentalized bento boxes or stackable containers to separate different components of your lunch and prevent flavors from mingling.

One popular option for a portable lunch is the classic sandwich or wrap. Choose a variety of fresh and wholesome bread or tortilla wraps as the base. Fill them with an assortment of flavorful ingredients like sliced vegetables, plant-based proteins, spreads, and condiments. Some tasty combinations include hummus and roasted vegetable wraps, tofu and avocado sandwiches, or chickpea salad pitas. These handheld meals are convenient, customizable, and perfect for enjoying on the go.

Salads are another fantastic choice for a portable lunch. Build your salad with a variety of leafy greens or grains as the foundation, then add a colorful assortment of vegetables, proteins, and dressings. Mason jar salads are a popular option, as the layers keep the ingredients crisp and prevent sogginess. Begin with the dressing at the bottom, followed by sturdy vegetables like cherry tomatoes or cucumbers, proteins like tofu or chickpeas, and finally, delicate greens or grains at the top. When ready to eat, simply shake the jar to distribute the dressing and enjoy a fresh and satisfying salad.

Portable soups or stews are comforting options for cooler days. Prepare a hearty and flavorful soup or stew packed with vegetables, legumes, and spices. Pour it into a thermos or insulated container to keep it warm. Pair it with crusty bread or crackers for a complete meal on the go. Popular choices include lentil soup, vegetable chili, or minestrone. These warm and nourishing options provide a comforting lunch experience wherever you are.

For a twist on the traditional lunch box, consider creating a DIY snack box or a grazing board-style lunch. Fill a divided container with an assortment of bite-sized snacks such as raw vegetables, whole-grain crackers, dips, hummus, fruits, nuts, and plant-based cheeses. This option allows you to enjoy a variety of flavors and textures while keeping your lunch light and portable.

Leftovers from the previous night's dinner can also make for a convenient and flavorful portable lunch. Cook extra portions of your favorite dishes, such as stir-fries, curries, or grain bowls, and pack them into microwave-safe containers. Simply reheat your leftovers at work or school for a satisfying and fuss-free lunch.

By incorporating portable lunch ideas into your routine, you can enjoy a delicious and nutritious meal wherever your day takes you. These convenient options allow you to savor your lunch break or snack time, even when you're on the move. So, pack your favorite ingredients, assemble your portable lunch with care, and savor the satisfaction of a nourishing meal, no matter where you are.

Portable lunch ideas have revolutionized the way we enjoy meals on the go, offering convenience, variety, and nutrition in one package. These practical and flavorful meals are designed to be easily packed and carried, ensuring that you can indulge in a satisfying lunch wherever your busy schedule takes you. Whether you're heading to the office, going to school, embarking on a road trip, or enjoying a day outdoors, incorporating portable lunch ideas allows you to savor a delicious and nourishing meal without sacrificing time or taste.

When it comes to crafting portable lunches, versatility and functionality are key. Begin by selecting ingredients that are not only tasty but also travel well. Opt for sturdy containers that are leak-proof and tightly sealed to keep your meal fresh and secure during transportation. Consider using compartmentalized lunch boxes or stackable containers to separate different components and prevent flavors from blending together.

A classic and reliable option for a portable lunch is the beloved sandwich or wrap. Choose your favorite type of bread or tortilla as the foundation and layer it with an array of flavorful fillings. From sliced vegetables and plant-based proteins to spreads and condiments, the possibilities are endless. Some delightful combinations include avocado and chickpea wraps, tempeh BLTs, or Mediterranean-inspired hummus and roasted vegetable sandwiches. These handheld delights are easy to assemble, customizable to your preferences, and perfect for enjoying on the move.

Salads are another fantastic choice for a portable lunch. Build a vibrant and nutritious salad using a variety of leafy greens, grains, or pasta as the base. Then, add a colorful assortment of vegetables, proteins, and dressings. Mason jar salads have gained popularity for their convenience and ability to keep ingredients fresh. Begin by pouring your dressing at the bottom, followed by sturdy vegetables like cherry tomatoes or cucumbers, proteins such as grilled tofu or chickpeas, and finally, delicate greens or grains on top. When it's time to eat, simply shake the jar to distribute the dressing and enjoy a refreshing and satisfying salad.

When the weather calls for something warm and comforting, portable soups or stews are the way to go. Prepare a hearty and flavorful soup or stew packed with vegetables, legumes, and aromatic spices. Pour it into a thermos or insulated container to keep it piping hot. Pair it with a side of crusty bread or crackers for a complete and comforting meal on the go. Popular options include lentil soup, vegetable curry, or a flavorful minestrone. These soul-soothing choices provide a cozy lunch experience no matter where you are.

For a unique twist on the traditional lunch box, consider creating a DIY snack box or a grazing board-style lunch. Fill a divided container with an assortment of bite-sized snacks such as raw vegetables, whole-grain crackers, dips like hummus or guacamole, fruits, nuts, and plant-based cheeses. This option allows you to enjoy a variety of flavors and textures while keeping your lunch light and easily transportable. It's a perfect choice for those who prefer to graze throughout the day or want to sample a range of delicious bites.

Leftovers from the previous night's dinner can also be transformed into a convenient and flavorful portable lunch. Cook extra portions of your favorite dishes, such as stir-fries, curries, or grain bowls, and pack them into microwave-safe containers. Simply reheat your leftovers at work or school, and you'll have a satisfying and hassle-free lunch that saves both time and effort.

Portable lunch ideas have transformed the way we approach midday meals, providing us with a convenient and versatile solution to enjoy delicious and nourishing food on the go. These carefully curated meals are designed to be easily packed and carried, allowing us to savor a satisfying lunch no matter where our busy lives take us. Whether you're headed to the office, going on a hike, or simply looking for a quick and convenient option, incorporating portable lunch ideas ensures that you can enjoy a flavorful and well-rounded meal without compromising on taste or nutrition.

When it comes to crafting portable lunches, creativity and practicality are key. Start by selecting ingredients that are not only delicious but also suitable for transportation. Opt for containers that are sturdy, leak-proof, and well-sealed to keep your meal fresh and intact. Consider using compartmentalized lunch boxes or stackable containers to separate different components and prevent flavors from mingling.

A classic and reliable option for a portable lunch is the timeless sandwich or wrap. Choose your preferred type of bread or tortilla as the foundation and layer it with an array of flavorful fillings. From fresh vegetables and plant-based proteins to spreads and condiments, the possibilities are endless. Whether you opt for a hearty tempeh and avocado sandwich or a refreshing Mediterranean-inspired wrap with hummus and crisp veggies, these handheld delights are easy to assemble and perfect for enjoying on the move.

Salads are another fantastic choice for a portable lunch, offering a refreshing and nutritious option. Build your salad with a base of leafy greens, grains, or pasta, and then add a colorful medley of vegetables, proteins, and dressings. Mason jar salads have gained popularity for their ability to keep ingredients fresh and crisp. Simply layer your favorite dressing at the bottom, followed by sturdy veggies like cherry tomatoes or cucumbers, proteins such as grilled tofu or chickpeas, and finally, delicate greens or grains on top. When it's time to eat, give the jar a gentle shake to combine the flavors and enjoy a delicious and well-balanced salad.

When you're in the mood for something warm and comforting, portable soups or stews are a wonderful choice. Prepare a hearty and flavorful soup or stew packed with vegetables, legumes, and aromatic spices. Pour it into a thermos or insulated container to keep it piping hot until lunchtime. Pair it with a side of crusty bread or crackers for a complete and satisfying meal. Whether you prefer a comforting lentil soup, a fragrant vegetable curry, or a robust minestrone, these portable options provide a cozy and nourishing lunch experience.

For a creative twist on the traditional lunch box, consider assembling a DIY snack box or a grazing-style lunch. Fill a divided container with an assortment of bite-sized snacks like raw vegetables, whole-grain crackers, hummus or guacamole dips, fresh fruits, nuts, and plant-based cheeses. This allows you to enjoy a diverse range of flavors and textures while keeping your lunch light and easy to transport. It's a perfect option for those who enjoy grazing throughout the day or want to sample a variety of delicious bites.

Leftovers from the previous night's dinner can also be transformed into a delightful and convenient portable lunch. Cook extra portions of your favorite dishes, such as stir-fries, curries, or grain bowls, and pack them into microwave-safe containers. When lunchtime arrives, simply reheat your leftovers and enjoy a flavorful and hassle-free meal that saves both time and effort.

To keep your portable lunch experience exciting, consider incorporating small treats or snacks like energy balls, granola bars, or fresh fruit for a touch of sweetness or a midday pick-me-up. These additional treats add a burst of flavor and keep your energy levels up throughout the day.

Travel-Friendly Snacks and Treats

Travel-friendly snacks and treats are essential for keeping you energized and satisfied while on the go. Whether you're embarking on a road trip, flying to a new destination, or simply running errands, having a selection of portable and delicious snacks ensures that you can curb hunger and indulge in a tasty treat wherever your travels take you. These convenient options are easy to pack, require little to no preparation, and provide a delightful pick-me-up during your journey.

When it comes to selecting travel-friendly snacks and treats, consider options that are not only delicious but also have a good shelf life and are resistant to heat or crushing. Opt for single-serving portions or pre-portioned snacks to ensure convenience and easy consumption. Additionally, choose snacks that provide a balance of nutrients, offering a mix of carbohydrates, protein, and healthy fats to keep you satiated and energized.

One classic option for travel-friendly snacking is a selection of nuts and seeds. These nutrient-dense powerhouses are packed with protein, fiber, and healthy fats, providing a satisfying and nourishing snack. Choose a variety of your favorites, such as almonds, walnuts, cashews, or pumpkin seeds, and portion them into individual snack bags or small containers. For added variety and flavor, consider adding dried fruits like raisins or cranberries, or even a sprinkle of dark chocolate chips.

Another popular choice for travel-friendly snacks is a mix of dried fruits and trail mix. Dried fruits like apricots, mangoes, or apples offer natural sweetness and provide a boost of vitamins and minerals. Combine them with a selection of nuts, seeds, and even some whole-grain pretzels or cereal for a satisfying and crunchy trail mix. This combination offers a great balance of carbohydrates, protein, and healthy fats to keep you fueled throughout your journey.

For those with a sweet tooth, portable energy bars or granola bars are a fantastic option. Look for bars made with whole food ingredients like oats, nuts, seeds, and dried fruits. These bars often provide a good balance of carbohydrates, protein, and healthy fats, making them a satisfying and convenient snack. Choose bars with minimal added sugars and without any artificial additives or preservatives.

Fresh fruits are also a wonderful choice for travel-friendly snacks. Apples, oranges, grapes, and bananas are all easy to transport and require no preparation. They provide natural sweetness, hydration, and a variety of vitamins and minerals. If you prefer to enjoy sliced fruits, consider packing them in a small, sealed container to keep them fresh and prevent them from getting crushed.

When it comes to treats, opt for individually wrapped chocolates, energy balls, or homemade granola bites. These bite-sized indulgences offer a sweet reward and a burst of energy. If you have dietary restrictions, look for vegan or gluten-free options to cater to your specific needs.

Don't forget the importance of hydration during your travels. Carry a reusable water bottle and fill it up whenever you have the opportunity. Staying hydrated is essential for maintaining energy levels and overall well-being.

Lastly, if you prefer savory snacks, consider packing individual packs of air-popped popcorn, roasted chickpeas, or veggie chips. These options provide a satisfying crunch while offering a healthier alternative to traditional chips.

When it comes to being on the move, having travel-friendly snacks and treats is essential to keep you fueled and satisfied. Whether you're embarking on a long road trip, exploring a new city, or simply commuting to work, having a selection of portable and delicious snacks ensures that you can indulge in a tasty treat wherever you go. These convenient options are easy to pack, require little to no preparation, and provide a delightful pick-me-up during your travels.

When choosing travel-friendly snacks and treats, consider options that are not only tasty but also have a good shelf life and are resistant to heat, crushing, or melting. Look for snacks that are individually wrapped or portioned into single servings for convenience and easy consumption on the go. Additionally, aim for snacks that offer a balance of nutrients, including carbohydrates, protein, and healthy fats, to provide sustained energy and satiation.

One go-to option for travel-friendly snacking is a selection of nuts and seeds. These nutritious powerhouses are rich in protein, fiber, and healthy fats, making them an excellent choice for sustained energy. Choose a variety of your favorites, such as almonds, cashews, pistachios, or sunflower seeds, and portion them into small snack bags or containers. They're compact, don't require refrigeration, and provide a satisfying crunch.

Another popular choice for travel-friendly snacking is a mix of dried fruits and trail mix. Dried fruits like apricots, cherries, or cranberries offer natural sweetness and provide a dose of vitamins and minerals. Combine them with a mixture of nuts, seeds, and perhaps some dark chocolate or coconut flakes for added flavor and texture. This homemade trail mix is not only delicious but also offers a good balance of carbohydrates, protein, and healthy fats for sustained energy.

Energy bars or granola bars are convenient and satisfying treats that are perfect for travel. Look for bars made with whole food ingredients like oats, nuts, seeds, and dried fruits. These bars often provide a good balance of macronutrients and are easily portable. Choose bars with minimal added sugars and without any artificial additives or preservatives.

Fresh fruits are a refreshing and nutritious option for travel-friendly snacking. Apples, bananas, grapes, or berries are easy to pack and require no preparation. They provide natural sweetness, hydration, and a variety of vitamins and minerals. Keep them in a small container or a reusable produce bag to prevent bruising or damage.

For those with a sweet tooth, individual servings of dark chocolate, fruit leathers, or rice cakes with nut butter can satisfy cravings while providing a quick energy boost. These treats are compact and won't easily melt or crumble during travel.

Savory snacks are also a great option for travel-friendly treats. Consider packing single-serve packets of whole-grain crackers, rice cakes, or vegetable chips. These options offer a satisfying crunch and can be enjoyed on their own or paired with individual hummus or nut butter packs.

Hydration is essential during travel, so don't forget to pack a reusable water bottle and refill it whenever you have the chance. Staying hydrated keeps your energy levels up and helps you feel refreshed throughout your journey.

By having a variety of travel-friendly snacks and treats on hand, you can maintain your energy levels and satisfy your cravings while on the go. These convenient options ensure that you're prepared for any hunger pangs or snack attacks that may arise, allowing you to focus on enjoying your travels or daily activities with ease.

Healthy Meals for Busy Weeknights

Finding time to prepare healthy meals during busy weeknights can be a challenge, but with a little planning and some quick and nutritious recipes, it's absolutely possible to enjoy wholesome meals that nourish your body and satisfy your taste buds. These meals are designed to be simple, flavorful, and require minimal time and effort, making them perfect for those hectic evenings when you're short on time but still want to enjoy a nutritious dinner.

One option for a quick and healthy weeknight meal is a stir-fry. Start by sautéing a mix of fresh vegetables like bell peppers, broccoli, carrots, and snap peas in a hot skillet with a small amount of oil. Add protein sources such as tofu, tempeh, or sliced chicken or beef, and season with soy sauce or a stir-fry sauce of your choice. Serve over cooked quinoa or brown rice for a complete and satisfying meal.

Another option is a sheet pan dinner. Simply place a variety of chopped vegetables like sweet potatoes, Brussels sprouts, and zucchini on a baking sheet, drizzle with olive oil, and season with herbs and spices. Roast in the oven until the vegetables are tender and slightly caramelized. Pair the roasted veggies with a protein source like baked salmon or chicken breast for a well-rounded and flavorful meal.

One-pot meals are also a great choice for busy weeknights. Prepare a hearty vegetable and bean soup by combining your favorite vegetables, such as tomatoes, onions, carrots, and spinach, in a large pot with vegetable broth and canned beans. Season with herbs and spices, and let it simmer until the flavors meld together. Serve with a side of whole-grain bread for a comforting and nourishing dinner.

If you're looking for a lighter option, consider making a salad with a twist. Start with a bed of fresh greens like spinach or mixed salad greens and top with a variety of colorful vegetables, such as cherry tomatoes, cucumbers, and grated carrots. Add protein sources like grilled chicken, chickpeas, or tofu. Sprinkle with seeds or nuts for added crunch and flavor. Drizzle with a homemade vinaigrette made from olive oil, vinegar, and your choice of herbs and spices. This simple yet satisfying salad provides a balance of nutrients and can be customized to suit your preferences.

For a quick and protein-packed meal, try a nourishing grain bowl. Cook a batch of your favorite whole grains like quinoa, brown rice, or bulgur. Top with roasted or sautéed vegetables, a protein source like grilled shrimp, baked tofu, or beans, and a flavorful sauce or dressing. Garnish with fresh herbs, chopped nuts, or avocado slices for added texture and taste. Grain bowls are not only nutritious but also highly customizable and can be made ahead of time for convenience.

Another option is a quick and delicious wrap or sandwich. Choose a whole-grain wrap or bread and fill it with a combination of lean protein like turkey or grilled chicken, plenty of fresh vegetables, and a spread or dressing of your choice. Add avocado slices, hummus, or mustard for extra flavor. This portable and balanced meal can be assembled in minutes and enjoyed on the go.

Meal prepping can also be a lifesaver for busy weeknights. Take some time during the weekend to prepare a batch of cooked grains, roasted vegetables, and grilled proteins. Store them in separate containers in the fridge, and when it's time for dinner, simply combine the prepped ingredients to create a quick and nutritious meal.

By incorporating these quick and healthy meal ideas into your busy weeknights, you can enjoy nourishing dinners that don't sacrifice taste or nutrition. With a little planning and some creativity, you can make weeknight meals a breeze. Here are a few more ideas for healthy meals:

Buddha bowls: Assemble a colorful and nutrient-packed bowl with a variety of cooked grains, roasted or sautéed vegetables, leafy greens, and a protein source like grilled tofu or chickpeas. Drizzle with a flavorful sauce or dressing for a satisfying and well-rounded meal.

Zucchini noodles (zoodles): Spiralize zucchini into noodle-like strands and sauté them with garlic and olive oil. Top with your favorite sauce, such as marinara or pesto, and add cooked vegetables or protein like sautéed mushrooms or grilled shrimp for a low-carb and veggie-filled dinner.

Quick and easy tacos: Fill whole-grain tortillas with your choice of protein, such as grilled fish, shredded chicken, or black beans. Top with fresh salsa, avocado slices, and a sprinkle of cheese. Serve with a side of roasted sweet potato wedges for a delicious and balanced meal.

Quinoa or couscous salad: Cook quinoa or couscous according to package instructions and let it cool. Toss with a mix of chopped vegetables, such as cucumbers, cherry tomatoes, and bell peppers. Add a protein source like grilled chicken or feta cheese, and dress with a light vinaigrette or lemon juice for a refreshing and filling salad.

Veggie-packed pasta: Cook whole-grain pasta according to package instructions and toss it with a medley of sautéed vegetables like zucchini, bell peppers, and spinach. Add a splash of olive oil, herbs, and a sprinkle of Parmesan cheese for a simple and satisfying pasta dish.

Stuffed bell peppers: Cut the tops off bell peppers and remove the seeds. Fill the peppers with a mixture of cooked quinoa, black beans, corn, and diced tomatoes. Top with shredded cheese and bake until the peppers are tender and the cheese is melted for a flavorful and nutritious meal.

Omelets or frittatas: Whip up a quick and protein-packed omelet or frittata with your choice of vegetables, such as mushrooms, spinach, and onions. Add in some diced tofu, tempeh, or shredded chicken for an extra boost of protein. Serve with a side of whole-grain toast for a hearty and satisfying dinner.

Remember, the key to preparing healthy meals on busy weeknights is to keep things simple, utilize time-saving techniques like prepping ingredients in advance, and focus on using fresh, whole foods. By making nutritious choices and being mindful of portion sizes, you can enjoy delicious and wholesome meals that support your well-being even during the busiest of evenings.

Prepping and Packing Vegan Meals

Prepping and packing vegan meals in advance can be a game-changer for those with busy schedules or those who want to ensure they have nourishing and delicious meals ready to go. By dedicating some time to meal prepping, you can streamline your cooking process and have convenient, ready-to-eat meals throughout the week. Whether you're preparing meals for work, school, or travel, prepping and packing vegan meals allows you to maintain a healthy and plant-based lifestyle even on the busiest of days.

The first step in prepping and packing vegan meals is to plan your meals for the week. Take some time to brainstorm recipes or ideas that you would like to incorporate into your meal prep. Consider recipes that are versatile, can be made in bulk, and have ingredients that can be easily stored and reheated. Think about including a variety of grains, legumes, vegetables, and plant-based proteins to ensure a balanced and satisfying meal.

Once you have your meal ideas, make a detailed grocery list and gather all the necessary ingredients. Shop for fresh produce, whole grains, legumes, nuts, and any other vegan staples you need for your meals. Having all the ingredients on hand will make the prepping process much smoother.

Next, carve out a designated time to cook and assemble your meals. This could be on a weekend or a day when you have a few hours to spare. Start by cooking large batches of grains like quinoa, brown rice, or farro. These can serve as the base for a variety of meals and can be easily reheated.

While the grains are cooking, prepare a selection of roasted or steamed vegetables. Chop and season them with herbs, spices, and a drizzle of olive oil. Roasting vegetables like sweet potatoes, broccoli, and bell peppers enhances their flavors and creates delicious meal components.

Another useful tip is to batch cook proteins such as tofu, tempeh, or lentils. Marinate and bake or pan-fry the tofu or tempeh, or cook a large pot of lentils that can be used in salads, stir-fries, or wraps throughout the week. This way, you have a protein source ready to go and can easily incorporate it into different meals.

To add more variety, prepare some sauces, dressings, or dips that can be used to flavor your meals. Make a batch of hummus, tahini sauce, or a vibrant vinaigrette to drizzle over salads or use as a dipping sauce for vegetables. These homemade condiments can elevate the flavors of your meals and add a touch of freshness.

Once everything is cooked and ready, it's time to portion and pack your meals. Invest in a set of reusable containers that are the right size for your meal portions. Start by dividing your grains into individual containers or sectioning them off into compartments. Add a generous serving of roasted vegetables, protein, and any additional toppings or sauces. Label the containers with the meal names or ingredients to make it easier to grab and go.

If you prefer to have more variety, you can opt for a meal prep bowl approach. Prepare multiple containers with different components like grains, roasted vegetables, protein, and sauces. Each day, you can mix and match these components to create a unique and satisfying meal.

Remember to keep your prepped meals properly refrigerated to maintain freshness and food safety. If you're planning to take your meals on the go, invest in an insulated lunch bag or cooler to keep them at the appropriate temperature.

By prepping and packing vegan meals in advance, you save time, reduce stress, and ensure that you have wholesome and satisfying meals readily available. Plus, by controlling the ingredients and portions, you have complete control over the nutritional content of your meals. Here are a few more tips to enhance your prepping and packing routine:

Use versatile Ingredients: Choose ingredients that can be used in multiple recipes throughout the week. For example, cook a large batch of chickpeas or black beans that can be added to salads, wraps, or grain bowls.

Make use of freezer-friendly options: Some meals, like soups, stews, and casseroles, can be prepared in larger quantities and frozen in individual portions. This allows you to have a variety of meals on hand that can be easily thawed and reheated when needed.

Embrace Mason jar salads: Layer your salad ingredients in Mason jars, starting with the dressing at the bottom, followed by hearty vegetables, grains, protein, and finally, leafy greens. This keeps the ingredients fresh and prevents them from becoming soggy. When ready to eat, simply shake the jar to distribute the dressing and enjoy a crisp and flavorful salad.

Consider snack packs: Pack small containers or snack-sized bags with a mix of nuts, dried fruits, seeds, or homemade energy balls. These individual portions make for convenient and nutritious snacks on the go.

Repurpose leftovers creatively: Transform leftovers from dinner into a new and exciting lunch the next day. For example, use roasted vegetables and protein from a previous meal to create a wrap, sandwich, or grain bowl. Add fresh ingredients and a drizzle of dressing for a unique and satisfying meal.

Don't forget about breakfast and snacks: Prepping meals goes beyond lunch and dinner. Consider preparing overnight oats, chia pudding, or smoothie packs for quick and nutritious breakfasts. Prep snack options like cut-up fruits and vegetables, homemade granola bars, or single-serving packs of nut butter to keep you fueled throughout the day.

Stay organized with a meal prep planner: Use a meal prep planner or calendar to map out your meals for the week, including prepping days, cooking times, and storage instructions. This helps you stay organized and ensures you have a variety of meals ready to enjoy.

Remember, the key to successful prepping and packing is finding a routine that works for you. Start with simple recipes and gradually expand your repertoire as you become more comfortable. Experiment with flavors, textures, and combinations to keep your meals exciting and enjoyable. With a little planning and preparation, you can enjoy healthy and delicious vegan meals throughout the week, no matter how busy your schedule may be.

Chapter 7: Veganism for Families and Kids

Raising Vegan Children

Raising vegan children is a personal choice that requires thoughtful planning, attention to nutrition, and open communication. With proper guidance and awareness, a vegan diet can provide all the necessary nutrients for children to thrive and grow. Here's a flowing and continuous explanation of raising vegan children:

Educate yourself: Before embarking on a vegan lifestyle for your children, educate yourself about plant-based nutrition, including the key nutrients needed for their growth and development. Understand the potential challenges and how to address them to ensure their nutritional needs are met.

Consult a healthcare professional: It's essential to consult with a pediatrician or registered dietitian who is knowledgeable about plant-based nutrition. They can provide guidance, monitor your child's growth and development, and make recommendations specific to their individual needs.

Ensure a balanced diet: A well-planned vegan diet can provide all the necessary nutrients for children. Focus on a variety of whole foods such as fruits, vegetables, whole grains, legumes, nuts, and seeds. Include sources of key nutrients like protein, calcium, iron, omega-3 fatty acids, and vitamin B12. Consider supplementation, particularly for vitamin B12, as it is primarily found in animal products.

Protein sources: Ensure your child receives adequate protein by including plant-based sources such as beans, lentils, tofu, tempeh, seitan, quinoa, and edamame. Offer a variety of protein-rich foods to meet their needs.

Calcium and vitamin D: Include plant-based sources of calcium, such as fortified plant-based milks, tofu, tempeh, leafy greens like kale and broccoli, and calcium-fortified foods. Ensure adequate vitamin D intake through sunlight exposure or vitamin D supplementation, as this vitamin is crucial for calcium absorption.

Iron-rich foods: Plant-based iron sources include dark leafy greens, legumes, fortified cereals, tofu, and dried fruits. Enhance iron absorption by pairing these foods with sources of vitamin C, like citrus fruits or bell peppers.

Omega-3 fatty acids: Include plant-based sources of omega-3s, such as ground flaxseeds, chia seeds, hemp seeds, walnuts, and algae-based supplements, to support brain and eye health. Consider discussing with a healthcare professional about the need for an algae-based omega-3 supplement for children.

Variety and supplementation: Encourage your child to try a wide variety of fruits, vegetables, grains, and legumes to ensure they receive a diverse array of nutrients. If necessary, work with a healthcare professional to determine if specific supplements are needed, such as vitamin B12 or iron.

Teach and empower: Educate your child about the reasons behind your vegan lifestyle and help them understand the importance of nutrition and making ethical choices. Encourage them to participate in meal planning, grocery shopping, and food preparation to foster their connection with plant-based foods.

Address social situations: Prepare your child for social situations where their vegan choices may differ from others.

Teach them how to communicate their dietary needs with respect and confidence. Encourage them to pack vegan snacks or meals when attending events where vegan options may be limited.

Monitor growth and development: Regularly monitor your child's growth and development through visits to a pediatrician. Keep track of their nutrient intake and seek professional guidance if any concerns arise.

Remember, raising vegan children involves more than just their diet. It encompasses teaching compassion, respect for animals and the environment, and promoting a balanced and healthy lifestyle overall. By fostering open communication, providing appropriate nutrition, and seeking guidance from professionals, you can raise thriving and well-nourished vegan children.

Kid-Friendly Vegan Lunches and Snacks

Sandwiches and Wraps: Create delicious and nutritious sandwiches and wraps using vegan-friendly fillings. Opt for spreads like hummus, avocado, or nut butter, and include kid-friendly fillings such as sliced cucumbers, cherry tomatoes, shredded carrots, or plant-based deli slices. Use whole-grain bread or tortillas for added fiber and nutrients.

Veggie and Dip Platter: Kids love to dip! Prepare a colorful platter of fresh vegetables like carrot sticks, celery, bell pepper strips, and cherry tomatoes. Pair them with vegan-friendly dips like hummus, guacamole, or dairy-free ranch dressing. It's a fun and nutritious way to get them excited about eating their veggies.

Bento Boxes: Bento boxes are a great way to offer a variety of kid-friendly foods in one convenient container. Fill the compartments with a mix of bite-sized fruits, veggie sticks, whole-grain crackers, plant-based cheese cubes, and a small portion of protein-rich foods like chickpeas or tofu cubes. Make it visually appealing by arranging the different components in an appealing manner.

Pasta Salad: Whip up a colorful and flavorful pasta salad using whole-grain pasta shapes. Toss cooked pasta with diced vegetables like cherry tomatoes, cucumbers, bell peppers, and olives. Add protein sources like cooked chickpeas, diced tofu, or plant-based deli slices. Dress it with a light vinaigrette or vegan mayo for a delicious and filling lunch option.

Veggie Sushi Rolls: Get creative with veggie sushi rolls by using nori seaweed sheets, sushi rice, and a variety of kid-friendly fillings. Include thinly sliced avocado, cucumber, carrot sticks, and even mango strips. Roll them up tightly and slice into bite-sized pieces. Serve with soy sauce or a dairy-free dipping sauce for a fun and nutritious lunch.

Fruit Kebabs: Skewer colorful fruit chunks onto wooden or reusable skewers for a visually appealing and tasty snack. Use a mix of seasonal fruits like melon, berries, grapes, pineapple, and kiwi. You can also add a dollop of dairy-free yogurt for dipping.

Energy Balls: Prepare homemade energy balls using ingredients like dates, nuts, seeds, and rolled oats. Blend them together, shape them into bite-sized balls, and refrigerate for a quick and satisfying snack. Customize the flavors by adding cocoa powder, shredded coconut, or dried fruits.

Smoothies: Blend together a refreshing and nutrient-packed smoothie using a variety of fruits, a plant-based milk, and a handful of leafy greens like spinach or kale. Add a scoop of nut butter or chia seeds for added protein and healthy fats. You can also freeze the smoothie into popsicle molds for a fun frozen treat.

Trail Mix: Create a homemade trail mix using a mix of dried fruits, nuts, and seeds. Combine dried cranberries, raisins, banana chips, almonds, cashews, sunflower seeds, and pumpkin seeds. Portion it into small snack bags for a convenient and satisfying on-the-go snack.

Mini Veggie Pizza: Make mini veggie pizzas using whole-grain English muffins or mini pitas as the base. Let your child top them with tomato sauce, plant-based cheese, and their favorite vegetables like sliced bell peppers, mushrooms, and cherry tomatoes. Bake until the cheese is melted and bubbly, and serve as a fun and customizable lunch option.

Remember to involve your children in the preparation process and make it enjoyable for them. By offering a variety of colorful and tasty options, you can introduce them to a diverse range of flavors and encourage their participation in making healthy food choices. Additionally, consider the following tips to make vegan lunches and snacks more appealing to kids:

Food Shapes and Skewers: Use cookie cutters to create fun shapes out of sandwiches, fruit slices, or vegan cheese. Kids often enjoy eating food that looks visually appealing. Skewer fruits, veggies, and plant-based protein sources like tofu or seitan to make eating more interactive and enjoyable.

Mini Pancakes or Waffles: Prepare mini pancakes or waffles using a vegan batter. You can add mashed bananas, blueberries, or grated carrots to the batter for added flavor and nutrition. Serve them with a side of maple syrup or fruit compote for a delightful breakfast-inspired lunch.

Crunchy Snacks: Kids love crunchy snacks! Offer air-popped popcorn, baked veggie chips, or roasted chickpeas as a healthier alternative to traditional potato chips. You can even make your own crispy kale chips by baking seasoned kale leaves until they turn crispy.

Fruit Salsa and Cinnamon Tortilla Chips: Dice a variety of fresh fruits like apples, strawberries, and mangoes to create a colorful fruit salsa. Serve it with homemade cinnamon tortilla chips made from whole-grain tortillas brushed with a little oil, sprinkled with cinnamon and sugar, and baked until crispy.

Vegan Yogurt Parfait: Layer vegan yogurt with a mix of fresh fruits, granola, and a drizzle of nut butter or honey alternative. This creates a tasty and nutritious parfait that can be enjoyed as a snack or even as a dessert.

Veggie Sticks with Hummus Faces: Cut carrot sticks, cucumber slices, and bell pepper strips into different shapes. Arrange them on a plate to create fun "hummus faces." Use hummus as the glue to stick the veggies together, and encourage your child to create their own edible artwork.

Frozen Fruit Pops: Blend together a mix of fruits and plant-based milk to create a smoothie mixture. Pour it into popsicle molds and freeze until solid. These fruity popsicles make for a refreshing and healthy treat during warmer months.

Veggie Quesadillas: Make veggie-packed quesadillas using whole-grain tortillas. Fill them with sautéed bell peppers, onions, corn, and black beans. Sprinkle with vegan cheese and fold them over. Cook until the tortilla is crispy and the cheese is melted. Serve with a side of salsa or guacamole.

Sweet Potato Fries: Bake sweet potato wedges until they're crispy on the outside and tender on the inside. Season with herbs and spices like paprika, garlic powder, and a pinch of salt. Serve as a tasty and nutritious alternative to regular fries.

Fruit and Veggie Smoothie Bowls: Blend together a thick and creamy smoothie using frozen fruits, plant-based milk, and a handful of spinach or kale. Pour it into a bowl and top with fresh fruit slices, granola, and a drizzle of nut butter. This makes for a satisfying and colorful snack.

Remember to tailor the options to your child's preferences and introduce new foods gradually. By making vegan lunches and snacks fun, delicious, and visually appealing, you can encourage your children to embrace a plant-based lifestyle while ensuring they receive the necessary nutrients for their growth and development.

Family-Friendly Dinner Ideas

Veggie-loaded Pasta: Prepare a comforting pasta dish by sautéing a medley of vegetables like bell peppers, zucchini, mushrooms, and spinach. Toss them with your choice of pasta, a flavorful tomato sauce, and a sprinkle of vegan cheese or nutritional yeast. Serve with a side salad or garlic bread for a well-rounded meal.

Build-Your-Own Tacos: Set up a taco bar with an array of fillings and toppings. Offer soft or crispy taco shells, and provide options like seasoned black beans, sautéed vegetables, diced tomatoes, guacamole, salsa, and vegan sour cream. Let each family member customize their tacos to their liking.

Veggie Stir-Fry: Whip up a quick and colorful stir-fry using an assortment of veggies like broccoli, carrots, snap peas, and bell peppers. Sauté them in a flavorful sauce made from soy sauce, ginger, garlic, and a touch of sweetener. Add tofu, tempeh, or edamame for a protein boost. Serve over steamed rice or noodles for a satisfying dinner.

Baked Potato Bar: Prepare a baked potato bar with a variety of toppings. Bake potatoes until tender, and set out an array of toppings such as vegan chili, steamed broccoli, sautéed mushrooms, diced tomatoes, vegan cheese, chives, and vegan sour cream. Let everyone create their own loaded potato masterpiece.

Lentil Shepherd's Pie: Make a hearty lentil shepherd's pie by cooking lentils with vegetables in a rich tomato-based sauce. Top it with a layer of mashed potatoes and bake until golden and bubbly. This comforting dish is packed with protein, fiber, and flavor.

Quinoa and Veggie Stuffed Peppers: Stuff bell peppers with a flavorful mixture of cooked quinoa, sautéed vegetables, and plant-based protein like black beans or lentils. Bake until the peppers are tender and the filling is heated through. Serve with a side salad for a nutritious and satisfying meal.

Veggie Pizza Night: Get the whole family involved in making homemade pizzas. Provide pre-made pizza dough or individual pizza crusts and let each family member choose their own toppings. Offer a variety of veggies, vegan cheese, and marinara sauce. Bake until the crust is crispy and the cheese is melted.

Chickpea Curry: Create a flavorful chickpea curry by simmering chickpeas in a fragrant blend of spices, coconut milk, and tomato sauce. Add vegetables like cauliflower, carrots, and peas for added texture and nutrition. Serve over steamed rice or with naan bread for a delicious and filling dinner.

Veggie Burgers: Grill or pan-fry homemade or store-bought veggie burgers and serve them on whole-grain buns. Offer an assortment of toppings like lettuce, tomato slices, pickles, onions, and condiments. Serve with oven-baked fries or a side salad for a classic and satisfying meal.

One-Pot Pasta Primavera: Cook pasta in a single pot with a medley of spring vegetables like asparagus, cherry tomatoes, and baby spinach. Add vegetable broth, herbs, and spices for flavor. Finish with a squeeze of lemon juice and a sprinkle of vegan Parmesan cheese for a quick and tasty dinner.

Remember to involve your family in the meal planning and preparation process. Let them choose their favorite recipes, help with chopping or stirring, and encourage them to try new flavors and ingredients. By making dinner an interactive and enjoyable experience, you create lasting memories and foster a love for healthy and delicious food among your family members.

Exploring Veganism with Teens

Exploring veganism with teens can be an exciting and educational journey. Here's a flowing and continuous explanation of how to approach veganism with teenagers:

Open Communication: Start by having open and honest conversations with your teen about veganism. Discuss the reasons behind your interest in veganism, such as animal welfare, environmental sustainability, or health benefits. Listen to their thoughts and concerns, and create a supportive and non-judgmental environment for exploration.

Educate Together: Explore veganism as a family by learning about plant-based nutrition, ethical considerations, and environmental impact. Watch documentaries, read books, or browse reputable online resources together to gather information and broaden your understanding of veganism.

Involve Teens in Meal Planning: Engage your teenager in meal planning and decision-making. Let them explore plant-based recipes, suggest their favorite dishes, and get involved in grocery shopping and meal preparation. Encourage them to express their preferences and experiment with new ingredients and flavors.

Cooking and Culinary Skills: Encourage your teen to develop their culinary skills by trying out vegan recipes. Support them in learning basic cooking techniques, such as chopping, sautéing, and baking. Involve them in the kitchen, giving them opportunities to experiment and explore their creativity with plant-based ingredients.

Encourage Independence: Allow your teen to make independent choices regarding their vegan journey. Let them explore plant-based options when dining out or socializing with friends. Support them in finding vegan-friendly alternatives and guide them in making informed decisions about food choices in various settings.

Nutritional Awareness: Ensure your teen understands the importance of a balanced and varied vegan diet. Teach them about essential nutrients like protein, iron, calcium, omega-3 fatty acids, and vitamin B12, and how to incorporate them into their meals. Encourage them to pay attention to portion sizes and to listen to their body's hunger and fullness cues.

Addressing Social Situations: Help your teen navigate social situations where their vegan choices may differ from others. Discuss strategies for dining out or attending social events, such as researching vegan-friendly restaurants, bringing vegan dishes to share, or respectfully communicating their dietary preferences with friends and family.

Supportive Community: Connect your teen with vegan communities or groups where they can interact with peers who share similar interests. Online platforms, local vegan meetups, or youth-focused vegan organizations can provide a supportive space for sharing experiences, exchanging ideas, and finding support.

Encourage Critical Thinking: Encourage your teen to critically evaluate information and sources related to veganism. Help them differentiate between evidence-based knowledge and misinformation. Teach them the importance of informed decision-making and critical thinking skills.

Celebrate Milestones: Acknowledge and celebrate milestones and achievements along their vegan journey. This can include trying a new vegan recipe, successfully navigating a social situation, or embracing veganism as a long-term lifestyle choice. Celebrating these milestones can boost your teen's confidence and motivation.

Remember, the exploration of veganism should be a positive and empowering experience for your teen. Focus on creating a supportive environment, fostering open communication, and promoting education and independent decision-making. By engaging your teen in the process, you can help them develop a strong foundation for a compassionate and sustainable lifestyle.

Chapter 8: Vegan for Fitness and Sports Performance

Fueling Your Workouts with Plant-Based Foods

Pre-Workout Nutrition: Prior to your workout, it's important to provide your body with the energy it needs to perform at its best. Opt for easily digestible carbohydrates, such as a banana, a slice of whole-grain toast with nut butter, or a homemade energy bar made with dates, oats, and nuts. These foods provide a quick source of energy to fuel your workout.

Hydration: Proper hydration is key for optimal performance. Drink water throughout the day leading up to your workout and continue to hydrate during your exercise session. If engaging in intense or prolonged workouts, consider adding electrolyte-rich beverages like coconut water or homemade sports drinks to replenish essential minerals lost through sweat.

During-Workout Snacks: For longer workouts, you may need to refuel with easily digestible snacks. Fresh or dried fruits, such as grapes or dates, can provide a quick energy boost. Homemade energy gels made with chia seeds, maple syrup, and fruit puree are also convenient options. Sip on water or a sports drink to stay hydrated during longer workouts.

Post-Workout Recovery: After your workout, it's important to replenish your energy stores and aid in muscle recovery. Aim for a balanced meal or snack that includes a combination of carbohydrates and protein. Whole-grain toast with avocado and tempeh, a quinoa salad with roasted vegetables and chickpeas, or a protein-packed smoothie with fruits and plant-based protein powder are all excellent choices.

Protein for Muscle Repair: Protein is crucial for muscle repair and growth. Include plant-based protein sources like tofu, tempeh, legumes, quinoa, nuts, and seeds in your post-workout meals. These foods provide essential amino acids and support muscle recovery.

Nutrient-Dense Meals: Focus on consuming nutrient-dense meals that include a variety of colorful fruits, vegetables, whole grains, and plant-based proteins. Incorporate leafy greens, berries, and cruciferous vegetables for their antioxidants and anti-inflammatory properties. Include whole grains like brown rice or quinoa for sustained energy, and choose plant-based proteins like lentils or beans for muscle repair.

Healthy Fats: Don't forget about incorporating healthy fats into your meals. Avocado, nuts, seeds, and plant-based oils like olive oil or coconut oil can provide essential fatty acids that support energy production and joint health.

Timing and Portion Control: Consider the timing of your meals and snacks in relation to your workout. Aim to eat a balanced meal or snack about 1-3 hours before exercise, allowing enough time for digestion. Post-workout, try to consume a meal or snack within 30 minutes to two hours to support muscle recovery.

Experiment and Listen to Your Body: Every individual is unique, so pay attention to how different foods and eating patterns affect your performance and recovery. Experiment with different plant-based foods and combinations to find what works best for you. Consider keeping a food and exercise journal to track your energy levels, performance, and any noticeable changes.

Consider Professional Guidance: If you have specific performance or nutrition goals, or if you're engaging in intense training, it may be helpful to consult with a registered dietitian who specializes in sports nutrition. They can provide personalized guidance based on your specific needs and help optimize your plant-based diet for athletic performance.

Remember, fueling your workouts with plant-based foods requires a balanced approach and attention to your individual needs. By incorporating nutrient-dense plant-based foods, staying hydrated, and timing your meals appropriately, you can optimize your workouts, support muscle recovery, and enhance your overall athletic performance.

Fueling your workouts with plant-based foods is a sustainable and nutritious approach to athletic performance. Plant-based diets provide an abundance of essential nutrients, antioxidants, and fiber that can support your energy levels, muscle recovery, and overall well-being. By incorporating a variety of plant-based foods into your meals and snacks, you can optimize your workouts and enhance your athletic performance.

Pre- and Post-Workout Nutrition for Vegans

Pre-Workout Nutrition: Prior to your workout, it's essential to provide your body with the right fuel to optimize performance and sustain energy levels. As a vegan, you can choose from a variety of plant-based options. Focus on consuming a balanced meal or snack that includes complex carbohydrates, a moderate amount of protein, and minimal fat.

Complex Carbohydrates: Opt for whole-food sources of carbohydrates like whole grains (oats, quinoa, brown rice), starchy vegetables (sweet potatoes, squash), or fruits. These provide a steady release of energy, helping to sustain your workout intensity.

Protein: Include a moderate amount of plant-based protein to support muscle repair and growth. Good sources include legumes (chickpeas, lentils, black beans), tofu, tempeh, seitan, or plant-based protein powders. Consider combining them with complex carbohydrates for a balanced meal or snack.

Minimal Fat: Keep fat intake minimal before workouts since it slows down digestion and can cause discomfort. Avoid high-fat foods like oils, heavy nut butters, or fatty snacks in your pre-workout meal.

Timing: Aim to consume your pre-workout meal or snack 1-3 hours before exercising to allow for digestion. This will vary depending on your individual tolerance, so find the timing that works best for you.

Post-Workout Nutrition: After your workout, your body requires nutrients to repair muscles, replenish glycogen stores, and optimize recovery. As a vegan, you can choose plant-based options rich in protein, carbohydrates, and essential nutrients.

Protein for Muscle Repair: Include a quality source of plant-based protein to aid in muscle repair and recovery. This can be in the form of legumes, tofu, tempeh, edamame, seitan, or plant-based protein powders. Aim for around 20-30 grams of protein within the first hour or two after your workout.

Complex Carbohydrates: Replenish glycogen stores by consuming complex carbohydrates like whole grains, fruits, or starchy vegetables. These help restore energy levels and support recovery.

Nutrient-Dense Foods: Opt for nutrient-dense options that provide vitamins, minerals, and antioxidants to aid in overall recovery. Include a variety of fruits, vegetables, and leafy greens to support immune function and reduce inflammation.

Hydration: Don't forget to hydrate post-workout. Drink water and consider adding electrolyte-rich fluids like coconut water or sports drinks to replenish electrolytes lost through sweat.

Timing: Aim to consume your post-workout meal or snack within 30 minutes to two hours after exercising to optimize recovery. This window is when your body is most receptive to replenishing nutrients.

Balanced Meal or Snack: Strive for a balanced meal or snack that includes a combination of carbohydrates and protein. For example, a post-workout smoothie made with plant-based protein powder, fruits, and a handful of leafy greens can be a quick and convenient option.

Remember, individual needs may vary depending on factors such as exercise intensity, duration, and personal goals. Experiment with different food combinations and timing to find what works best for you. If you have specific performance goals or concerns, consider consulting a registered dietitian who specializes in sports nutrition to create a personalized plan that meets your needs as a vegan athlete.

By paying attention to your pre- and post-workout nutrition as a vegan, you can optimize your energy levels, support muscle recovery, and enhance your overall athletic performance.

Building Muscle on a Vegan Diet

Building muscle on a vegan diet is not only possible but also highly achievable with careful planning and attention to nutrition. By focusing on plant-based protein sources, consuming adequate calories, and incorporating strength training into your fitness routine, you can effectively build lean muscle mass.

Plant-Based Protein Sources: As a vegan, there are numerous protein-rich plant-based options available to support muscle growth. Include a variety of legumes (such as lentils, chickpeas, and black beans), soy products (like tofu and tempeh), seitan, edamame, quinoa, hemp seeds, chia seeds, and plant-based protein powders in your diet. These sources provide essential amino acids necessary for muscle repair and growth.

Calorie Surplus: To build muscle, it's important to consume a slight calorie surplus. Ensure you're consuming enough calories to meet your energy needs, including the additional calories required for muscle growth. Focus on nutrient-dense foods like whole grains, fruits, vegetables, nuts, and seeds to provide the necessary energy for workouts and recovery.

Strength Training: Incorporate strength training exercises into your fitness routine to stimulate muscle growth. Focus on compound exercises such as squats, deadlifts, bench presses, shoulder presses, and rows. Progressive overload, gradually increasing the weight or resistance used, will help challenge your muscles and promote growth.

Post-Workout Nutrition: After strength training, prioritize post-workout nutrition to support muscle recovery and growth. Consume a combination of carbohydrates and protein within 30 minutes to two hours after your workout. Include a plant-based protein source like tofu, tempeh, or a protein-rich smoothie with plant-based protein powder. Pair it with complex carbohydrates like whole grains, fruits, or starchy vegetables for optimal nutrient delivery.

Meal Planning and Timing: Plan your meals and snacks to ensure you're consuming adequate protein throughout the day. Spread your protein intake evenly across meals to support muscle protein synthesis. Aim for 20-30 grams of protein per meal, depending on your individual needs and goals. Incorporate protein-rich snacks like edamame, chickpea hummus, or protein bars throughout the day.

Micronutrient Considerations: While focusing on protein, don't overlook the importance of other nutrients. Ensure you're meeting your needs for vitamins, minerals, and essential fatty acids through a well-rounded plant-based diet. Include a variety of fruits, vegetables, whole grains, and healthy fats to support overall health and well-being.

Hydration: Stay adequately hydrated as it plays a crucial role in muscle function and recovery. Drink water throughout the day and consider adding electrolyte-rich beverages like coconut water or natural sports drinks during intense workouts to replenish electrolytes lost through sweat.

Rest and Recovery: Allow your body time to rest and recover between workouts. Aim for 7-8 hours of quality sleep each night to promote optimal recovery and muscle growth. Incorporate active recovery days, stretching, and self-care practices to support overall well-being.

Professional Guidance: If you're new to strength training or have specific muscle-building goals, consider seeking guidance from a qualified fitness professional or registered dietitian who specializes in sports nutrition. They can provide personalized advice, meal planning support, and help you optimize your vegan diet for muscle growth.

By focusing on plant-based protein sources, consuming enough calories, and engaging in regular strength training, you can effectively build muscle on a vegan diet. Consistency, proper nutrition, and progressive overload in your workouts are key factors in achieving your muscle-building goals. Remember, individual needs may vary, so listen to your body, make adjustments as necessary, and celebrate your progress along the way. With dedication and a well-planned vegan diet, you can achieve the muscle-building results you desire.

Progressive Overload: Gradually increase the intensity, volume, or resistance in your strength training exercises over time. This progressive overload stimulates muscle adaptation and growth. Keep challenging yourself with heavier weights, more repetitions, or advanced exercise variations to continue making progress.

Adequate Carbohydrates: Don't neglect carbohydrates in your muscle-building journey. They provide energy for intense workouts and aid in muscle glycogen replenishment. Include complex carbohydrates like whole grains, sweet potatoes, quinoa, and brown rice in your meals to fuel your training sessions and support recovery.

Healthy Fats: Include sources of healthy fats in your diet to support hormone production, joint health, and overall well-being. Incorporate foods like avocados, nuts, seeds, and plant-based oils such as olive oil or flaxseed oil. These fats also help with nutrient absorption and provide satiety.

Meal Timing: Consider distributing your protein intake evenly throughout the day to support muscle protein synthesis. Aim to consume protein-rich foods at each meal and snack. Spacing your meals with protein evenly helps maximize muscle recovery and growth.

Supplement Considerations: While not necessary, certain supplements may support your muscle-building efforts. Vegan protein powders, creatine monohydrate, and branched-chain amino acids (BCAAs) are commonly used by athletes to enhance muscle growth and recovery. However, it's important to consult with a healthcare professional or registered dietitian before adding any supplements to your regimen.

Patience and Consistency: Building muscle takes time, so be patient with the process. Consistency in your workouts, nutrition, and recovery practices is key. Stay dedicated to your training program, maintain a well-rounded vegan diet, and prioritize rest and recovery for optimal results.

Tracking Progress: Keep track of your workouts, strength gains, and body composition changes. This allows you to monitor your progress and make adjustments as needed. Take measurements, photos, or keep a training journal to see how far you've come and stay motivated.

Listen to Your Body: Pay attention to how your body responds to different training methods and dietary choices. Everyone's needs and preferences are unique, so adjust your approach based on how you feel, perform, and recover. Fine-tune your diet and training regimen to suit your individual needs and goals.

Supportive Community: Surround yourself with like-minded individuals who share your passion for veganism and fitness. Join online communities, connect with vegan athletes, or find workout buddies who can provide support, motivation, and guidance along your muscle-building journey.

Remember, building muscle on a vegan diet requires a comprehensive approach that encompasses proper nutrition, consistent training, rest, and recovery. By focusing on plant-based protein sources, consuming adequate calories, and following a well-structured strength training program, you can achieve your desired muscle-building goals while adhering to your vegan principles. Stay committed, be patient, and celebrate your progress as you work towards building a strong, healthy, and muscular physique.

Vegan Athletes and Success Stories

Vegan athletes have been making significant strides in various sports, debunking the myth that animal products are necessary for optimal athletic performance. Their achievements showcase the potential of a plant-based diet in fueling and supporting athletic endeavors. Let's explore some success stories and notable vegan athletes across different disciplines:

Scott Jurek: An ultramarathon runner, Scott Jurek is a well-known vegan athlete who has won multiple ultramarathons, including the prestigious Western States Endurance Run. He credits his plant-based diet for enhancing his endurance, recovery, and overall health.

Venus Williams: A legendary tennis player, Venus Williams adopted a vegan diet to manage an autoimmune condition. Despite the challenges, she continues to excel in her sport and credits her plant-based lifestyle for improved energy levels and recovery.

Patrik Baboumian: Patrik Baboumian is a record-breaking strongman who holds multiple world records in various weightlifting categories. He is known for his incredible strength and power while following a vegan diet. His achievements highlight the potential of plant-based nutrition in building and maintaining muscle mass.

Fiona Oakes: A long-distance runner and marathoner, Fiona Oakes holds several world records in marathon running. She has been a vegan since her teenage years and believes her plant-based lifestyle has contributed to her endurance and overall well-being.

Morgan Mitchell: Morgan Mitchell, an Australian sprinter, competed in the 2016 Olympic Games while following a vegan diet. She believes that plant-based nutrition has helped her maintain energy levels, recover faster, and support her athletic performance.

Derrick Morgan: Derrick Morgan, a former NFL player, transitioned to a vegan diet during his professional football career. He found that it improved his recovery, reduced inflammation, and contributed to his overall health and longevity.

Tia Blanco: Tia Blanco is a professional surfer who has achieved remarkable success while following a vegan lifestyle. She advocates for the benefits of plant-based nutrition in optimizing athletic performance and sustaining the health of both individuals and the planet.

These are just a few examples of vegan athletes who have thrived on plant-based diets while excelling in their respective sports. Their success stories demonstrate that a well-planned vegan diet can provide the necessary nutrients to support athletic performance, including sufficient protein, carbohydrates, and micronutrients.

It's important to note that each athlete's journey and dietary needs may vary based on factors such as sport, individual genetics, and training goals. However, these success stories illustrate that plant-based nutrition can be a viable and effective choice for athletes seeking to optimize their performance and achieve their goals.

Whether in endurance sports, strength-based activities, or team sports, vegan athletes continue to inspire and challenge the notion that animal products are essential for athletic success.

Their accomplishments highlight the potential of plant-based nutrition in fueling athletic endeavors and contributing to overall health and well-being.

If you're an aspiring vegan athlete or considering adopting a plant-based lifestyle, it's beneficial to work with a registered dietitian who specializes in sports nutrition. They can help you create a personalized meal plan that meets your nutritional needs and supports your athletic goals while following a vegan diet.

Remember, the power of plant-based nutrition and the achievements of vegan athletes serve as a testament to the effectiveness and benefits of this lifestyle choice in the realm of sports and athleticism.

Chapter 9: Vegan Beauty and Personal Care

Cruelty-Free and Vegan Cosmetics

Cruelty-free and vegan cosmetics are products that are developed and manufactured without harming animals and without using any animal-derived ingredients. They are an ethical and sustainable choice for those who value animal welfare and want to support a compassionate and cruelty-free beauty industry. Let's explore this concept further:

Cruelty-Free Certification: Cruelty-free cosmetics are products that have not been tested on animals at any stage of their development, including individual ingredients and finished products. These products are certified by recognized organizations such as Leaping Bunny, PETA, or Choose Cruelty-Free. Look for their logos or statements on packaging to ensure you are purchasing truly cruelty-free cosmetics.

Animal-Derived Ingredients: Vegan cosmetics go a step further by excluding any animal-derived ingredients from their formulations. These products do not contain substances like beeswax, lanolin, carmine (a red dye derived from insects), or animal-derived collagen. Instead, they use plant-based alternatives or synthetic substitutes to achieve similar effects.

Ethical Testing Methods: Instead of animal testing, cruelty-free and vegan cosmetic companies use alternative testing methods. These can include in vitro testing, computer modeling, and human volunteer studies to ensure safety and efficacy. This approach aligns with the belief that animals should not suffer for the sake of beauty and promotes the development of innovative and humane testing techniques.

Plant-Based Ingredients: Vegan cosmetics predominantly use plant-based ingredients derived from fruits, vegetables, nuts, seeds, botanicals, and minerals. These ingredients offer a wide range of benefits for the skin and can provide hydration, nourishment, and protection. Common examples include plant oils, shea butter, aloe vera, plant extracts, and natural pigments.

Environmental Impact: Choosing cruelty-free and vegan cosmetics is not only beneficial for animals but also for the environment. Animal agriculture, often associated with conventional cosmetic ingredients, can contribute to deforestation, greenhouse gas emissions, and water pollution. By opting for plant-based alternatives, you can reduce your ecological footprint and support a more sustainable beauty industry.

Transparency and Labels: Look for clear labeling on cosmetic products to ensure their cruelty-free and vegan status. Look for phrases like "cruelty-free," "vegan," or "not tested on animals" on the packaging. Recognized certification logos from cruelty-free organizations provide additional assurance of a product's ethical credentials.

Market Accessibility: The demand for cruelty-free and vegan cosmetics has grown significantly in recent years. As a result, there is now a wide range of options available across various price points, from drugstore to high-end brands. Many major beauty companies have also started offering cruelty-free and vegan product lines or have undergone a transition to become cruelty-free.

Consumer Empowerment: By choosing cruelty-free and vegan cosmetics, consumers send a powerful message to the beauty industry. Your purchasing decisions can drive change and encourage more companies to adopt ethical practices. Supporting cruelty-free and vegan brands and sharing your preferences with friends and family can create a positive ripple effect.

Online Resources: Various online resources, including websites and mobile apps, provide comprehensive databases and guides to help you navigate the world of cruelty-free and vegan cosmetics. These resources offer product recommendations, ingredient information, and updates on brands' cruelty-free and vegan status.

Remember, choosing cruelty-free and vegan cosmetics allows you to express your personal values while enjoying high-quality and effective beauty products. By opting for these ethical alternatives, you contribute to a more compassionate and sustainable beauty industry that respects the well-being of animals, the environment, and your own values.

DIY Vegan Skincare Recipes

DIY vegan skincare recipes are a wonderful way to personalize your beauty routine while ensuring that the products you use are free from animal-derived ingredients and cruelty-free. By creating your own skincare products with natural, plant-based ingredients, you can take control of what goes onto your skin and tailor the recipes to your specific skincare needs. Let's explore some popular DIY vegan skincare recipes:

Cleansing Oils: Make your own gentle and nourishing cleansing oil by combining plant-based oils such as jojoba oil, sweet almond oil, or grapeseed oil with a small amount of castor oil. This DIY recipe effectively removes makeup and dirt while leaving your skin hydrated and balanced.

Face Masks: Create a rejuvenating face mask by mixing mashed avocado, coconut milk, and a tablespoon of agave nectar. This mask provides hydration, antioxidants, and vitamins to revitalize and nourish your skin. You can also experiment with ingredients like oatmeal, cucumber, or turmeric to address specific skin concerns.

Body Scrubs: Combine granulated sugar or coffee grounds with a moisturizing oil like coconut oil or olive oil to make a luxurious exfoliating body scrub. Add a few drops of essential oils like lavender or citrus for a relaxing or invigorating scent. Gently massage the scrub onto damp skin to remove dead skin cells and reveal smoother, softer skin.

Facial Toners: Create a simple and refreshing facial toner by steeping chamomile or green tea in boiling water and allowing it to cool. Transfer the tea to a spray bottle and add a few drops of witch hazel or rose water. Spritz the toner onto your face after cleansing to hydrate and balance your skin.

Lip Balms: Make your own nourishing lip balm by melting together plant-based waxes (such as candelilla wax or carnauba wax), moisturizing oils like shea butter or cocoa butter, and a few drops of your favorite essential oil for fragrance. Pour the mixture into small containers and let it solidify. This DIY lip balm will keep your lips soft and hydrated.

Moisturizers: Combine aloe vera gel, vegetable glycerin, and a few drops of a lightweight plant-based oil like grapeseed or jojoba oil to create a hydrating and soothing moisturizer. Adjust the ratio based on your skin's needs to achieve your desired consistency.

Eye Creams: Make a DIY eye cream by blending together shea butter, almond oil, and a drop of vitamin E oil. This nourishing blend can help hydrate the delicate skin around your eyes and minimize the appearance of fine lines.

Face Serums: Create a customized face serum by combining different plant-based oils, such as rosehip oil, argan oil, and evening primrose oil. Add a few drops of essential oils like lavender or frankincense for added benefits and fragrance. This DIY face serum can provide hydration, antioxidants, and nutrients to promote healthy and radiant skin.

Remember to research and test the ingredients you use to ensure they are suitable for your skin type and any specific skin concerns you may have. It's also important to maintain proper hygiene and storage for your DIY skincare products to prevent contamination.

DIY vegan skincare recipes not only allow you to control the ingredients but also provide an opportunity to be creative and explore the benefits of natural plant-based ingredients. Enjoy the process of making your own personalized skincare products and embrace the nourishing and cruelty-free qualities of these homemade creations.

Navigating Vegan-Friendly Haircare and Body Products

Navigating vegan-friendly haircare and body products involves choosing products that are free from animal-derived ingredients and have not been tested on animals. By opting for vegan options, you can support ethical and cruelty-free beauty practices while maintaining healthy hair and skin. Here are some key points to consider:

Reading Labels: When selecting haircare and body products, read the labels carefully. Look for explicit statements such as "vegan," "cruelty-free," or "not tested on animals." Avoid products that contain animal-derived ingredients such as keratin, silk proteins, or animal-derived oils like lanolin or beeswax.

Plant-Based Ingredients: Vegan haircare and body products rely on plant-based ingredients to achieve desirable results. Look for nourishing plant oils like coconut, argan, or jojoba oil for hydration and hair/skin health. Natural botanical extracts, fruit extracts, and plant-based proteins provide beneficial properties without compromising vegan principles.

Synthetic Alternatives: Vegan products often utilize synthetic alternatives to replicate the benefits of animal-derived ingredients. For example, instead of using animal-derived collagen, vegan options may contain plant-based alternatives like hyaluronic acid or plant peptides to enhance skin hydration and firmness.

SLS and SLES-Free: Avoid products that contain Sodium Lauryl Sulfate (SLS) or Sodium Laureth Sulfate (SLES), as these ingredients can be derived from animal sources. Opt for sulfate-free formulas, which are gentler on the hair and skin while still effectively cleansing and maintaining moisture balance.

Ethical Certification: Look for certifications from recognized organizations such as Leaping Bunny, PETA, or Choose Cruelty-Free. These certifications ensure that the products have not been tested on animals and meet cruelty-free standards. These logos or statements are often displayed on the product packaging or brand websites.

Natural Fragrances: Many vegan haircare and body products use natural fragrances derived from plant extracts or essential oils. These scents offer a pleasant experience without the use of animal-derived ingredients or synthetic fragrances.

Environmentally Conscious Packaging: Consider brands that prioritize sustainable and eco-friendly packaging. Look for recyclable, biodegradable, or minimal packaging options to minimize your environmental impact.

Research and Reviews: Conduct research and read reviews about different vegan haircare and body product brands. Online resources, cruelty-free beauty blogs, and vegan lifestyle websites can provide helpful information and recommendations to assist in your decision-making process.

Brand Transparency: Support brands that are transparent about their vegan and cruelty-free practices. Look for brands that openly share their ingredient sourcing, manufacturing processes, and ethical commitments. Social media platforms and brand websites are great sources for learning more about a company's values and practices.

Personal Preferences: Each person's hair and skin have unique needs and sensitivities. Experiment with different vegan haircare and body products to find ones that work best for you. Adjust your routine based on factors such as hair type, skin type, and specific concerns.

By choosing vegan-friendly haircare and body products, you can align your personal care routine with your ethical values while promoting cruelty-free practices. Embrace the abundance of plant-based alternatives available and enjoy the benefits of nourishing and effective products that respect animals, the environment, and your own well-being.

Ethical Fashion: Vegan Clothing and Accessories

Ethical fashion encompasses a range of practices aimed at promoting sustainable, cruelty-free, and environmentally conscious clothing and accessories. Vegan fashion specifically focuses on products that are free from animal-derived materials and animal exploitation. By choosing vegan clothing and accessories, you can make fashion choices that align with your values and contribute to a more compassionate and sustainable industry. Let's explore this concept further:

Animal-Free Materials: Vegan fashion avoids the use of animal-derived materials such as leather, fur, silk, wool, and exotic skins. Instead, it embraces innovative and sustainable alternatives like plant-based fabrics, recycled materials, and synthetic fibers. Common animal-free materials include organic cotton, bamboo, hemp, cork, pineapple leather (Piñatex), and recycled polyester.

Cruelty-Free Production: Vegan fashion emphasizes ethical practices throughout the production process. It ensures that no animals are harmed, exploited, or subjected to inhumane treatment. This includes avoiding practices like factory farming, live plucking, mulesing, and cruel harvesting methods commonly associated with animal-based materials.

Sustainable Manufacturing: Ethical fashion, including vegan clothing and accessories, promotes sustainable manufacturing processes. This involves reducing waste, conserving water, using eco-friendly dyes and chemicals, and implementing fair labor practices. Many vegan fashion brands are committed to transparency and provide information about their supply chain and production methods.

Innovative Materials: Vegan fashion encourages the development and use of innovative and eco-friendly materials. This includes materials made from recycled plastics, organic and regenerative fibers, and upcycled or repurposed materials. These innovative alternatives help reduce the reliance on non-renewable resources and minimize environmental impact.

Fair Trade and Ethical Labor: Ethical fashion advocates for fair trade practices and ensures that workers involved in the production process are treated fairly, provided safe working conditions, and paid fair wages. Vegan fashion brands often partner with manufacturers and suppliers who follow these ethical standards, fostering positive social impact.

Transparency and Certifications: Many vegan fashion brands prioritize transparency by providing information about their materials, manufacturing processes, and supply chains. Look for certifications such as PETA's "Vegan Approved" or other recognized labels that confirm a brand's commitment to cruelty-free and vegan principles.

Fashion Forward Designs: Vegan fashion is not limited to a specific style or aesthetic. It encompasses a wide range of fashionable designs, from casual and minimalist to bold and statement-making. Vegan clothing and accessories can be as trendy, stylish, and versatile as their non-vegan counterparts, proving that fashion and ethics can coexist.

Consumer Empowerment: By supporting vegan fashion, consumers play a vital role in driving positive change within the fashion industry. Your purchasing choices can influence brands to shift towards more sustainable and cruelty-free practices, ultimately shaping a more compassionate and sustainable future for fashion.

Accessible and Diverse Options: Vegan clothing and accessories are becoming increasingly accessible, with a growing number of brands offering vegan options or fully embracing vegan principles. Whether shopping online, at specialized vegan boutiques, or in mainstream stores, you can find a wide range of vegan fashion choices to suit your style and preferences.

Personal Expression: Vegan fashion allows you to express your personal style and values simultaneously. Embrace the opportunity to curate a wardrobe that reflects your ethics while expressing your unique fashion sense. Mix and match different styles, experiment with colors and textures, and embrace the versatility of vegan fashion.

Choosing vegan clothing and accessories is an empowering way to make a positive impact on animal welfare, the environment, and the fashion industry as a whole. By supporting brands that align with your values, you contribute to the demand for cruelty-free and sustainable fashion.

Chapter 10: Vegan Ethics and Activism

Understanding Animal Rights and Liberation

Animal rights and liberation revolve around the ethical treatment and freedom of all animals. At its core, it recognizes that animals, across various species, are sentient beings capable of feeling pain, experiencing emotions, and exhibiting cognitive abilities. Advocates of animal rights and liberation challenge the exploitation, use, and harm inflicted upon animals for human purposes.

This concept is rooted in the belief that animals have inherent value and deserve to be treated with compassion and respect. It rejects the idea of animals as commodities or property, advocating for their freedom from practices such as factory farming, animal testing, fur farming, and other forms of exploitation that prioritize human interests over the well-being of animals.

Animal rights and liberation promote the ethical consideration of animals, encouraging individuals and society to question and challenge practices that cause harm to animals. It calls for nonviolence and compassion towards animals, urging people to adopt a vegan or plant-based lifestyle that avoids the use of animal products and supports cruelty-free alternatives.

Animal rights activism plays a crucial role in raising awareness and advocating for the rights and welfare of animals. Activists work to expose animal cruelty, promote animal-friendly legislation, and drive shifts towards a more compassionate society. They challenge the notion of speciesism, which asserts human superiority over other animal species, and instead call for equal consideration and respect for all sentient beings.

Conservation and habitat protection are also central to animal rights and liberation. Recognizing the importance of preserving natural habitats and protecting ecosystems, advocates promote sustainable practices and work towards the preservation of biodiversity. They understand that animals' well-being and survival depend on the conservation of their natural environments.

Animal rights and liberation intersect with other social justice movements, recognizing that the fight for animal rights is interconnected with issues such as environmental justice, human rights, and food justice. This understanding promotes collaboration and solidarity among different advocacy movements, amplifying the collective impact of social change efforts.

Legal and policy reforms are sought to protect animals and recognize their rights. Animal rights and liberation activists work towards strengthening animal welfare laws, advocating for the banning of cruel practices, and pushing for legislation that reflects the ethical consideration of animals.

Education and raising awareness are vital components of animal rights and liberation. By fostering a cultural shift towards a more compassionate and ethical relationship with animals, individuals and organizations strive to create positive change. They aim to promote alternatives to animal exploitation, encourage empathy and respect towards animals, and inspire others to adopt more ethical practices in their daily lives.

By supporting animal rights and liberation, individuals contribute to a more just and compassionate world for all sentient beings. It involves recognizing animals as individuals with inherent value, challenging oppressive practices, and promoting compassion and ethical considerations in our interactions with animals.

Effective Advocacy: Speaking Up for Animals

Effective advocacy involves using your voice and influence to speak up for animals and promote their rights and well-being. As an advocate, you play a crucial role in raising awareness, inspiring change, and working towards a more compassionate world.

Education and awareness form the foundation of effective advocacy. By educating yourself about animal rights, welfare issues, and the various forms of animal exploitation, you gain the knowledge necessary to advocate effectively. Stay informed about current events, research, and advancements in the field to address common misconceptions and engage in meaningful conversations.

To be an effective advocate, it's important to communicate your message clearly and concisely. Tailor your language and approach to your audience, whether it's friends, family, colleagues, or the broader public. Use factual information, personal stories, and compelling arguments to convey the ethical, environmental, and health reasons for advocating on behalf of animals.

Utilize various platforms to amplify your message. Social media, blogs, websites, and public speaking engagements offer opportunities to reach a wider audience and spark meaningful dialogue. Share educational content, thought-provoking articles, inspiring stories, and impactful visuals that highlight the importance of animal rights and the impact of our choices on animals' lives.

Collaborate with like-minded individuals and organizations to maximize your advocacy efforts. Join local or online animal rights groups, attend conferences and events, and participate in campaigns and initiatives. By working together, you can create a stronger collective voice and effect positive change on a larger scale.

Engage with policymakers and legislators to advocate for stronger animal welfare laws and policies. Write letters, make phone calls, and attend public hearings to voice your concerns and support initiatives that protect animals' rights and promote their well-being. Grassroots advocacy, combined with legislative action, can drive meaningful change at the societal level.

Lead by example through your own lifestyle choices. Adopt a vegan or plant-based diet, avoid products tested on animals, and opt for cruelty-free alternatives. By living in alignment with your values, you become a powerful advocate and inspire others to consider their impact on animals.

Lastly, practice empathy and compassion in your advocacy efforts. Recognize that not everyone may share your perspective, and approach conversations with patience and understanding. Encourage open dialogue and be willing to listen and address concerns. By fostering a compassionate and inclusive approach, you can create a more welcoming environment for discussions about animal rights.

By speaking up for animals, you contribute to a growing movement that seeks to end animal exploitation and create a more compassionate world. Your voice has the power to educate, inspire, and effect change. Embrace the opportunity to advocate for those who cannot speak for themselves and be a powerful force in the fight for animal rights.

Getting Involved: Volunteerism and Animal Sanctuaries

Getting involved through volunteerism and supporting animal sanctuaries is a powerful way to make a positive impact on the lives of animals. By dedicating your time, skills, and resources, you can directly contribute to the care, rehabilitation, and well-being of animals in need. Here's how you can get involved:

Volunteerism allows you to actively participate in animal welfare initiatives. Animal sanctuaries, rescue organizations, and animal rights groups often rely on dedicated volunteers to assist with various tasks. These can include animal care, feeding, grooming, cleaning enclosures, and providing socialization and enrichment activities for animals in their care.

Volunteering at animal sanctuaries provides an opportunity to connect with animals on a personal level. It allows you to witness their individual stories of resilience and recovery while offering them comfort and support. By offering your time and care, you can make a significant difference in the lives of animals who have experienced abuse, neglect, or abandonment.

Beyond direct animal care, volunteers can contribute their skills in areas such as fundraising, event planning, marketing, graphic design, photography, or website development. These skills are invaluable in helping organizations raise awareness, advocate for animal rights, and generate the necessary resources to support their missions.

Volunteerism also offers opportunities to engage with the local community and raise awareness about animal welfare issues. By participating in outreach events, educational programs, and public speaking engagements, you can spread compassion and knowledge, inspiring others to take action and make ethical choices that benefit animals.

Supporting animal sanctuaries financially is another impactful way to get involved. Donations and sponsorships contribute to the daily care, medical needs, and expansion of these safe havens for animals. Additionally, fundraising events, online crowdfunding campaigns, and partnerships with businesses or community organizations can help generate funds to support the ongoing operations and growth of sanctuaries.

By volunteering or supporting animal sanctuaries, you become part of a compassionate network dedicated to creating a better world for animals. Your involvement helps ensure that animals in need receive the care, love, and protection they deserve. It's an opportunity to make a tangible difference while fostering a deeper understanding of animal rights and the importance of coexistence with all sentient beings.

Whether you contribute your time, skills, or financial resources, getting involved through volunteerism and supporting animal sanctuaries is a meaningful way to create positive change. Your dedication and compassion have the power to transform the lives of animals, inspire others, and contribute to a more compassionate and ethical society.

Making a Difference: Donations and Supporting Animal Welfare Organizations

Making a difference through donations and supporting animal welfare organizations is a powerful way to contribute to the well-being and protection of animals. By providing financial support, resources, and raising awareness, you play a vital role in advancing animal rights and creating positive change. Here's how you can make a difference:

One impactful way to support animal welfare organizations is through monetary donations. Your financial contributions help fund rescue operations, veterinary care, rehabilitation programs, and the day-to-day operations of these organizations. Whether it's a one-time donation or a recurring monthly contribution, your generosity directly impacts the lives of animals in need.

In addition to financial contributions, you can also donate essential supplies, such as food, bedding, toys, and medical equipment. Many animal welfare organizations have wish lists or specific requests for items they need. By donating these supplies, you help ensure that animals receive the care and resources necessary for their well-being.

Supporting animal welfare organizations goes beyond monetary donations and supplies. You can also contribute by volunteering your time and skills. Offer your expertise in areas such as administration, marketing, event planning, or fundraising. Your skills can help organizations operate more efficiently, reach a broader audience, and raise the necessary funds to support their initiatives.

Another way to make a difference is by engaging in fundraising activities. Organize events, campaigns, or online fundraisers to raise funds for specific projects or causes. Collaborate with local businesses, schools, or community groups to maximize your impact. By mobilizing others to support animal welfare, you create a ripple effect of compassion and advocacy.

Raising awareness about animal welfare issues is crucial to effecting change. Utilize social media platforms, personal networks, and community spaces to share educational content, inspiring stories, and calls to action. By amplifying the voices of animals and shedding light on their plight, you help educate others and inspire compassionate choices.

Consider supporting or advocating for legislative initiatives that protect animal rights. Stay informed about animal welfare laws, sign petitions, and engage in letter-writing campaigns or public demonstrations to encourage policymakers to enact stronger protections for animals. Your voice, combined with collective action, can drive significant changes in legislation and policies.

Supporting animal welfare organizations also extends to making ethical choices in your own life. Adopting a vegan or plant-based lifestyle, avoiding products tested on animals, and promoting cruelty-free alternatives align with the values of animal welfare. By making conscious choices, you create a demand for more compassionate and sustainable practices in various industries.

Remember, every contribution, whether big or small, makes a difference. By donating, volunteering, raising awareness, and supporting animal welfare organizations, you actively participate in the movement to protect and advocate for animals. Together, we can create a more compassionate and ethical world, where animals are treated with dignity, respect, and compassion.

Vegan recipes to delight your palate

Breakfast recipes

Vegan Breakfast Burrito

Prep Time: 15 minutes | **Cook Time:** 15 minutes | Serves: 2

Ingredients:
4 large flour tortillas
1 cup firm tofu, crumbled
1/2 red bell pepper, diced
1/2 green bell pepper, diced
1/2 small red onion, diced
1/2 cup black beans, cooked
1/2 teaspoon ground cumin
1/2 teaspoon turmeric powder
1/2 teaspoon paprika
Salt and pepper to taste
2 tablespoons nutritional yeast
Handful of fresh cilantro, chopped
Salsa or hot sauce (optional)
Avocado slices for serving

Directions:
In a large skillet, heat some oil over medium heat. Add the diced bell peppers and red onion. Sauté until the vegetables are tender, about 5 minutes.

Add the crumbled tofu to the skillet, along with the cumin, turmeric, paprika, salt, and pepper. Cook for another 5 minutes, stirring occasionally to ensure even cooking.

Stir in the black beans and nutritional yeast. Cook for an additional 2 minutes until everything is well combined and heated through. Adjust the seasoning if needed.

Warm the flour tortillas in a separate skillet or microwave according to the package instructions.

To assemble the burritos, spoon the tofu and vegetable mixture onto each tortilla. Top with fresh cilantro and a drizzle of salsa or hot sauce, if desired.

Roll up the tortillas tightly, tucking in the sides as you go. Serve the vegan breakfast burritos with avocado slices on the side.

Nutrition: Calories: 340 | Fat: 8g | Carbohydrates: 47g | Fiber: 9g | Protein: 19g

Classic Vegan Pancakes

Prep Time: 10 minutes | **Cook Time:** 15 minutes | **Serve:** 4

Ingredients:
1 1/2 cups all-purpose flour
2 tablespoons sugar
2 teaspoons baking powder
1/2 teaspoon salt
1 1/4 cups plant-based milk (such as almond or soy milk)
2 tablespoons vegetable oil
1 teaspoon vanilla extract
Maple syrup and fresh fruits for serving

Directions:
In a large mixing bowl, whisk together the flour, sugar, baking powder, and salt.

In a separate bowl, combine the plant-based milk, vegetable oil, and vanilla extract. Stir well to combine.

Pour the wet ingredients into the dry ingredients and whisk until just combined. Be careful not to overmix; a few lumps are okay.

Heat a non-stick skillet or griddle over medium heat. Lightly grease the surface with oil or cooking spray.

Pour 1/4 cup of the pancake batter onto the skillet for each pancake. Cook until bubbles form on the surface, then flip and cook for an additional 1-2 minutes, or until golden brown.

Repeat with the remaining batter, adjusting the heat if needed to prevent burning.

Serve the pancakes warm with maple syrup and fresh fruits of your choice.

Nutrition: Calories: 210 | Fat: 6g | Carbohydrates: 34g | Fiber: 1g | Protein: 4g

Banana Walnut Pancakes

Prep Time: 10 minutes | **Cook Time:** 15 minutes | **Serve:** 2

Ingredients:
1 cup all-purpose flour
1 tablespoon sugar
2 teaspoons baking powder
1/2 teaspoon salt
1 ripe banana, mashed
3/4 cup plant-based milk (such as almond or oat milk)
1 tablespoon vegetable oil
1/2 teaspoon vanilla extract
1/4 cup chopped walnuts
Maple syrup and additional banana slices for serving

Directions:
In a large mixing bowl, whisk together the flour, sugar, baking powder, and salt.
In a separate bowl, combine the mashed banana, plant-based milk, vegetable oil, and vanilla extract. Stir well to combine.
Pour the wet ingredients into the dry ingredients and whisk until just combined. Be careful not to overmix; a few lumps are okay.
Gently fold in the chopped walnuts.
Heat a non-stick skillet or griddle over medium heat. Lightly grease the surface with oil or cooking spray.
Pour 1/4 cup of the pancake batter onto the skillet for each pancake. Cook until bubbles form on the surface, then flip and cook for an additional 1-2 minutes, or until golden brown.
Repeat with the remaining batter, adjusting the heat if needed to prevent burning.
Serve the pancakes warm with maple syrup and additional banana slices.

Nutrition: Calories: 290 | Fat: 10g | Carbohydrates: 44g | Fiber: 3g | Protein: 6g

Prep Time: 5 minutes | **Cook Time:** 0 minutes | **Serve:** 2

Ingredients:
1/4 cup chia seeds
1 cup plant-based milk (such as almond or coconut milk)
1 tablespoon maple syrup or other sweetener of choice
1/2 teaspoon vanilla extract
Fresh fruits, nuts, or seeds for topping

Directions:
In a bowl or jar, combine the chia seeds, plant-based milk, maple syrup, and vanilla extract.
Stir well to ensure the chia seeds are evenly distributed and not clumped together.
Cover the bowl or jar and refrigerate overnight or for at least 4 hours to allow the chia seeds to absorb the liquid and thicken into a pudding-like consistency.
After the chilling period, give the chia pudding a good stir to break up any clumps and ensure a smooth texture.
Serve the overnight chia pudding in bowls or glasses, and top with your choice of fresh fruits, nuts, or seeds.
Enjoy chilled and store any leftovers in the refrigerator for up to 3 days.

Nutrition: Calories: 180 | Fat: 8g | Carbohydrates: 20g | Fiber: 13g | Protein: 6g

Vegan Omelette

Prep Time: 10 minutes | **Cook Time:** 10 minutes | **Serve:** 1

Ingredients:
1/2 cup chickpea flour
1/2 cup water
1 tablespoon nutritional yeast
1/2 teaspoon turmeric powder
1/4 teaspoon garlic powder
Salt and pepper to taste

Fillings of your choice (e.g., sautéed vegetables, vegan cheese, spinach, mushrooms)
Fresh herbs for garnish (optional)
Salsa or hot sauce for serving (optional)

Directions:
In a mixing bowl, whisk together the chickpea flour, water, nutritional yeast, turmeric powder, garlic powder, salt, and pepper until well combined and no lumps remain. Let the batter rest for a few minutes to thicken slightly.
Heat a non-stick skillet over medium heat and lightly grease the surface with oil or cooking spray.
Pour the chickpea flour batter onto the skillet, spreading it evenly to form a thin layer.
Cook for about 3-4 minutes or until the edges start to firm up and the bottom is golden brown.
Flip the omelette carefully using a spatula and cook for another 2-3 minutes on the other side.
Once the omelette is cooked, transfer it to a plate and fill one half with your desired fillings.
Fold the other half over the fillings, creating a half-moon shape.
Garnish with fresh herbs, if desired, and serve with salsa or hot sauce on the side.

Nutrition: Calories: 210 | Fat: 5g | Carbohydrates: 27g | Fiber: 5g | Protein: 15g

Avocado Toast

Prep Time: 5 minutes | **Cook Time:** 0 minutes | **Serve:** 1

Ingredients:
1 ripe avocado
2 slices of whole grain bread
1 tablespoon lemon juice
Salt and pepper to taste
Optional toppings: sliced tomatoes, sprouts, nutritional yeast

Directions:
Slice the avocado in half, remove the pit, and scoop the flesh into a bowl.
Mash the avocado with a fork until it reaches your desired consistency.
Stir in the lemon juice and season with salt and pepper to taste.
Toast the slices of bread until golden brown.
Spread the mashed avocado onto the toast, dividing it evenly between the two slices.
Add any optional toppings you desire, such as sliced tomatoes, sprouts, or a sprinkle of nutritional yeast.
Serve the avocado toast immediately and enjoy!

Nutrition: Calories: 280 | Fat: 15g | Carbohydrates: 30g | Fiber: 10g | Protein: 6g

Vegan French Toast

Prep Time: 10 minutes | **Cook Time:** 10 minutes | **Serve:** 2

Ingredients:
4 slices of thick bread (such as French bread or sourdough)
1 cup plant-based milk (such as almond or soy milk)
2 tablespoons chickpea flour
1 tablespoon nutritional yeast
1 tablespoon maple syrup
1 teaspoon vanilla extract
1/2 teaspoon ground cinnamon
Coconut oil or vegan butter for cooking
Fresh fruits, maple syrup, and powdered sugar for serving

Directions:
In a shallow bowl, whisk together the plant-based milk, chickpea flour, nutritional yeast, maple syrup, vanilla extract, and ground cinnamon until well combined.
Heat a non-stick skillet or griddle over medium heat and lightly grease the surface with coconut oil or vegan butter.
Dip each slice of bread into the milk mixture, making sure to coat both sides evenly.

Place the soaked bread onto the skillet and cook for about 3-4 minutes on each side, or until golden brown and crispy.
Repeat with the remaining slices of bread, adding more oil or vegan butter as needed.
Serve the vegan French toast warm with fresh fruits, a drizzle of maple syrup, and a sprinkle of powdered sugar.

Nutrition: Calories: 230 | Fat: 5g | Carbohydrates: 38g | Fiber: 2g | Protein: 8g

Lunch Recipes

Prep Time: 15 minutes | **Cook Time:** 20 minutes | **Serve:** 2

Ingredients:
1 cup cooked quinoa or grain of choice
1 cup roasted sweet potatoes, diced
1 cup roasted chickpeas
2 cups mixed greens or baby spinach
1/2 cup cherry tomatoes, halved
1/2 cup cucumber, sliced
1/2 avocado, sliced
2 tablespoons hummus or tahini
Fresh lemon wedges (optional)
Salt and pepper to taste

Directions:
Start by preparing the roasted sweet potatoes and chickpeas if not already cooked. Preheat the oven to 400°F (200°C). Toss the sweet potatoes and chickpeas separately with a drizzle of olive oil, salt, and pepper. Roast the sweet potatoes for 20-25 minutes and the chickpeas for 15-20 minutes, or until crispy.
Assemble the Buddha bowls by dividing the cooked quinoa, roasted sweet potatoes, roasted chickpeas, mixed greens, cherry tomatoes, cucumber, and avocado into two serving bowls.
Drizzle each bowl with hummus or tahini and squeeze fresh lemon juice over the top, if desired.
Season with salt and pepper to taste.
Serve the vegan Buddha bowls immediately, and enjoy!

Nutrition: Calories: 450 | Fat: 18g | Carbohydrates: 60g | Fiber: 12g | Protein: 14g

Prep Time: 15 minutes | **Cook Time:** 0 minutes | **Serve:** 2

Ingredients:
1 can chickpeas, drained and rinsed
2 tablespoons vegan mayonnaise
1 tablespoon lemon juice
1/4 cup diced red onion
1/4 cup diced celery
1/4 cup chopped fresh parsley
Salt and pepper to taste
4 large lettuce leaves or tortillas
Sliced tomatoes, cucumbers, and avocado for filling

Directions:
In a medium bowl, mash the chickpeas with a fork or potato masher until partially mashed, leaving some whole chickpeas for texture.
Add the vegan mayonnaise, lemon juice, red onion, celery, parsley, salt, and pepper to the bowl. Stir well to combine.
Taste and adjust the seasonings as needed.
Lay out the lettuce leaves or tortillas and divide the chickpea salad mixture evenly among them.
Top with sliced tomatoes, cucumbers, and avocado.
Roll up the lettuce leaves or fold the tortillas to enclose the filling, creating a wrap.
Slice the wraps in half, if desired, and serve immediately.

Nutrition: Calories: 250 | Fat: 10g | Carbohydrates: 32g | Fiber: 10g | Protein: 9g

Lentil Soup

Prep Time: 10 minutes | **Cook Time:** 30 minutes | **Serve:** 4

Ingredients:
1 cup dried lentils (green or brown), rinsed
1 tablespoon olive oil
1 onion, chopped
2 carrots, diced

2 celery stalks, diced
3 cloves garlic, minced
1 teaspoon ground cumin
1 teaspoon ground turmeric
1/2 teaspoon ground paprika
4 cups vegetable broth
1 can diced tomatoes
1 bay leaf
Salt and pepper to taste
Fresh parsley or cilantro for garnish (optional)

Directions:
In a large pot, heat the olive oil over medium heat. Add the chopped onion, carrots, celery, and minced garlic. Sauté until the vegetables are tender, about 5 minutes.
Add the ground cumin, turmeric, and paprika to the pot. Stir well to coat the vegetables with the spices.
Add the rinsed lentils, vegetable broth, diced tomatoes (including the juice), and bay leaf to the pot. Stir to combine.
Bring the soup to a boil, then reduce the heat to low. Cover the pot and simmer for about 20-25 minutes, or until the lentils are tender.
Season the lentil soup with salt and pepper to taste.
Remove the bay leaf from the soup before serving.
Ladle the lentil soup into bowls and garnish with fresh parsley or cilantro, if desired.

Nutrition: Calories: 220 | Fat: 4g | Carbohydrates: 36g | Fiber: 12g | Protein: 12g

Vegan Caesar Salad

Prep Time: 15 minutes | **Cook Time:** 0 minutes | **Serve:** 2

Ingredients:
1 head of romaine lettuce, washed and torn into bite-sized pieces
1/2 cup vegan Caesar dressing (store-bought or homemade)
1/2 cup croutons (store-bought or homemade)
2 tablespoons nutritional yeast
1 tablespoon capers (optional)

Freshly ground black pepper to taste
Lemon wedges for serving

Directions:
Place the torn romaine lettuce in a large mixing bowl.
Pour the vegan Caesar dressing over the lettuce and toss well to coat all the leaves.
Add the croutons, nutritional yeast, and capers (if using) to the bowl. Toss again to distribute the toppings.
Season with freshly ground black pepper to taste.
Divide the vegan Caesar salad among serving plates or bowls.
Serve with lemon wedges on the side for squeezing over the salad, if desired.

Nutrition: Calories: 180 | Fat: 10g | Carbohydrates: 18g | Fiber: 5g | Protein: 5g

Sweet Potato and Black Bean Quesadilla

Prep Time: 15 minutes | **Cook Time:** 25 minutes | **Serve:** 2

Ingredients:
1 large sweet potato, peeled and diced
1/2 cup cooked black beans
1/2 red bell pepper, diced
1/4 red onion, diced
1 teaspoon ground cumin
1/2 teaspoon smoked paprika
Salt and pepper to taste
4 whole wheat tortillas
Vegan cheese, shredded (optional)
Guacamole or salsa for serving

Directions:
Preheat the oven to 400°F (200°C).
Place the diced sweet potato on a baking sheet and drizzle with olive oil. Sprinkle with cumin, smoked paprika, salt, and pepper. Toss to coat.
Roast the sweet potato in the preheated oven for about 20 minutes, or until tender and slightly caramelized.

In a large skillet, heat a little oil over medium heat. Add the diced red bell pepper and red onion. Sauté until softened, about 5 minutes.

Add the cooked black beans to the skillet and cook for another 2-3 minutes, until heated through. Season with salt, pepper, and additional spices if desired.

Place two tortillas on a clean surface. Divide the roasted sweet potato, black bean mixture, and vegan cheese (if using) evenly between the tortillas.

Top each with another tortilla.

Heat a large skillet or griddle over medium heat. Cook each quesadilla for about 2-3 minutes on each side, until golden brown and crispy.

Remove the quesadillas from the skillet and cut into wedges.

Serve the sweet potato and black bean quesadillas warm, accompanied by guacamole or salsa.

Nutrition: Calories: 350 | Fat: 6g | Carbohydrates: 65g | Fiber: 12g | Protein: 12g

Quinoa and Vegetable Stir-Fry

Prep Time: 15 minutes | **Cook Time:** 20 minutes | **Serve:** 2

Ingredients:
1 cup cooked quinoa
1 tablespoon vegetable oil
1 small onion, thinly sliced
2 cloves garlic, minced
1 carrot, julienned
1 red bell pepper, thinly sliced
1 zucchini, thinly sliced
1 cup broccoli florets
1 cup snap peas
2 tablespoons soy sauce (or tamari for gluten-free)
1 tablespoon maple syrup or agave nectar
1 tablespoon rice vinegar
1/2 teaspoon sesame oil
Sesame seeds for garnish (optional)

Directions:
Heat the vegetable oil in a large skillet or wok over medium heat.
Add the onion and garlic to the skillet and sauté for 2-3 minutes,
until the onion is translucent and fragrant.
Add the carrot, bell pepper, zucchini, broccoli, and snap peas to
the skillet. Stir-fry for 5-7 minutes, or until the vegetables are
tender-crisp.
In a small bowl, whisk together the soy sauce, maple syrup, rice
vinegar, and sesame oil. Pour the sauce over the vegetables in the
skillet.
Add the cooked quinoa to the skillet and toss everything together
to combine well. Continue to cook for an additional 2-3 minutes,
or until the quinoa is heated through.
Remove the skillet from the heat and sprinkle with sesame seeds
for garnish, if desired.
Serve the quinoa and vegetable stir-fry warm.

Nutrition: Calories: 320 | Fat: 8g | Carbohydrates: 54g | Fiber:
9g | Protein: 11g

Vegan Falafel Wrap

Prep Time: 20 minutes | **Cook Time:** 15 minutes | **Serve:** 2

Ingredients:
For the falafel:
1 can chickpeas, drained and rinsed
1/4 cup fresh parsley
1/4 cup fresh cilantro
1 small onion, chopped
3 cloves garlic
2 tablespoons flour (such as chickpea flour or all-purpose flour)
1 teaspoon ground cumin
1/2 teaspoon ground coriander
1/2 teaspoon salt
1/4 teaspoon black pepper
Oil for frying
For the wrap:
2 large tortilla wraps
Hummus

Sliced tomatoes
Sliced cucumbers
Shredded lettuce
Sliced red onion
Optional toppings: pickles, tahini sauce, hot sauce

Directions:
In a food processor, combine the chickpeas, parsley, cilantro, onion, garlic, flour, cumin, coriander, salt, and black pepper. Process until the mixture is well combined but still slightly chunky.
Form the falafel mixture into small patties, about 2 inches in diameter.
Heat a thin layer of oil in a frying pan over medium heat. Fry the falafel patties for about 3-4 minutes per side, or until golden brown and crispy. Transfer to a paper towel-lined plate to drain excess oil.
Warm the tortilla wraps in a dry skillet or microwave.
Spread a generous amount of hummus on each tortilla wrap.
Layer the sliced tomatoes, cucumbers, shredded lettuce, red onion, and falafel patties onto the wraps.
Add any optional toppings such as pickles, tahini sauce, or hot sauce.
Roll up the wraps tightly, tucking in the sides as you go.
Cut the wraps in half and serve immediately.

Nutrition: Calories: 380 | Fat: 10g | Carbohydrates: 60g | Fiber: 10g | Protein: 15g

Vegan Lentil Curry

Prep Time: 15 minutes | **Cook Time:** 30 minutes | **Serve:** 4

Ingredients:
1 tablespoon coconut oil
1 onion, chopped
3 cloves garlic, minced
1 tablespoon grated ginger
2 tablespoons curry powder
1 teaspoon ground cumin
1 teaspoon ground coriander
1/2 teaspoon turmeric
1/4 teaspoon cayenne pepper (optional for heat)
1 cup dried red lentils
1 can coconut milk
1 can diced tomatoes
2 cups vegetable broth
2 cups chopped vegetables (such as carrots, bell peppers, and spinach)
Salt and pepper to taste
Fresh cilantro for garnish (optional)
Cooked rice or naan bread for serving

Directions:
Heat the coconut oil in a large pot over medium heat.
Add the chopped onion, minced garlic, and grated ginger to the pot. Sauté until the onion is translucent and fragrant, about 5 minutes.
Add the curry powder, ground cumin, ground coriander, turmeric, and cayenne pepper (if using) to the pot. Stir well to coat the onion mixture with the spices.
Add the dried red lentils, coconut milk, diced tomatoes, and vegetable broth to the pot. Stir to combine.
Bring the mixture to a boil, then reduce the heat and let it simmer for about 20-25 minutes, or until the lentils are tender and cooked through.

Add the chopped vegetables to the pot and continue to simmer for an additional 5 minutes, or until the vegetables are cooked to your desired tenderness.
Season with salt and pepper to taste.
Garnish with fresh cilantro, if desired.
Serve the vegan lentil curry over cooked rice or with naan bread.

Nutrition: Calories: 320 | Fat: 10g | Carbohydrates: 45g | Fiber: 12g | Protein: 14g

Roasted Vegetable Medley

Prep Time: 15 minutes | **Cook Time:** 25 minutes | **Serve:** 4

Ingredients:
2 cups mixed vegetables (such as bell peppers, zucchini, eggplant, and cherry tomatoes), chopped
1 red onion, sliced
2 cloves garlic, minced
2 tablespoons olive oil
1 tablespoon balsamic vinegar
1 teaspoon dried herbs (such as thyme or rosemary)
Salt and pepper to taste
Fresh parsley for garnish (optional)

Directions:
Preheat the oven to 425°F (220°C).
In a large bowl, combine the mixed vegetables, sliced red onion, minced garlic, olive oil, balsamic vinegar, dried herbs, salt, and pepper. Toss to coat the vegetables evenly.
Spread the vegetable mixture on a baking sheet in a single layer.
Roast in the preheated oven for about 20-25 minutes, or until the vegetables are tender and slightly caramelized, stirring once or twice during cooking.
Remove from the oven and let the roasted vegetables cool for a few minutes.
Garnish with fresh parsley, if desired.
Serve the roasted vegetable medley as a side dish or as a topping for salads, wraps, or grain bowls.

Nutrition: Calories: 120 | Fat: 7g | Carbohydrates: 14g | Fiber: 4g | Protein: 2g

---

Vegan Bolognese with Zucchini Noodles

Prep Time: 15 minutes | **Cook Time:** 25 minutes | **Serve:** 4

Ingredients:
4 medium zucchini
2 tablespoons olive oil
1 onion, chopped
2 cloves garlic, minced
1 carrot, finely chopped
1 celery stalk, finely chopped
1 red bell pepper, chopped
1 can (14 oz) crushed tomatoes
1 can (14 oz) diced tomatoes
2 tablespoons tomato paste
1 teaspoon dried oregano
1 teaspoon dried basil
1/2 teaspoon dried thyme
Salt and pepper to taste
Fresh basil leaves for garnish (optional)

Directions:
Spiralize the zucchini into noodle-like strands using a spiralizer or julienne peeler. Set aside.
Heat the olive oil in a large pan over medium heat. Add the chopped onion, minced garlic, chopped carrot, celery, and red bell pepper. Sauté until the vegetables are softened, about 5 minutes.
Add the crushed tomatoes, diced tomatoes, tomato paste, dried oregano, dried basil, dried thyme, salt, and pepper to the pan. Stir well to combine.
Simmer the sauce for about 15-20 minutes, stirring occasionally, until it thickens and the flavors meld together.
While the sauce is simmering, heat a separate pan over medium heat. Add the zucchini noodles and cook for 3-4 minutes until slightly softened but still crisp.
Serve the zucchini noodles with the vegan bolognese sauce on top.

Garnish with fresh basil leaves, if desired.

Nutrition: Calories: 180 | Fat: 7g | Carbohydrates: 25g | Fiber: 7g | Protein: 6g

Prep Time: 10 minutes | **Cook Time:** 25 minutes | **Serve:** 4

Ingredients:
2 tablespoons olive oil
1 onion, diced
3 cloves garlic, minced
1 red bell pepper, diced
1 teaspoon ground cumin
1 teaspoon ground coriander
1/2 teaspoon smoked paprika
1/4 teaspoon cayenne pepper (adjust according to your spice preference)
1 can (14 oz) diced tomatoes
2 cups cooked chickpeas
2 cups vegetable broth
2 cups chopped spinach or kale
Salt and pepper to taste
Fresh cilantro for garnish (optional)
Cooked rice or crusty bread for serving

Directions:
Heat the olive oil in a large pot over medium heat. Add the diced onion, minced garlic, and diced red bell pepper. Sauté until the vegetables are softened, about 5 minutes.
Add the ground cumin, ground coriander, smoked paprika, and cayenne pepper to the pot. Stir well to coat the vegetables with the spices.
Pour in the diced tomatoes (including the juice) and add the cooked chickpeas and vegetable broth. Stir to combine.
Bring the stew to a simmer and let it cook for about 15 minutes, allowing the flavors to meld together.
Stir in the chopped spinach or kale and cook for an additional 5 minutes, or until the greens are wilted.

Season with salt and pepper to taste.

Garnish with fresh cilantro, if desired.

Serve the spicy chickpea stew over cooked rice or with crusty bread for dipping.

Nutrition: Calories: 230 | Fat: 8g | Carbohydrates: 32g | Fiber: 9g | Protein: 9g

Vegan Stir-Fried Tofu and Vegetables

Prep Time: 15 minutes | **Cook Time:** 15 minutes | **Serve:** 4

Ingredients:
1 block (14 oz) firm tofu, drained and cubed
2 tablespoons soy sauce or tamari
1 tablespoon cornstarch
2 tablespoons vegetable oil
1 onion, thinly sliced
2 cloves garlic, minced
1 bell pepper, thinly sliced
2 cups broccoli florets
1 carrot, thinly sliced
1 cup snap peas or snow peas
3 tablespoons stir-fry sauce
1 tablespoon sesame oil (optional)
Sesame seeds for garnish (optional)
Cooked rice or noodles for serving

Directions:
In a bowl, combine the cubed tofu, soy sauce or tamari, and cornstarch. Toss gently to coat the tofu evenly.

Heat the vegetable oil in a large skillet or wok over medium-high heat. Add the tofu and cook until golden brown and crispy on all sides. Remove from the skillet and set aside.

In the same skillet, add the sliced onion and minced garlic. Stir-fry for 2-3 minutes until the onion is translucent.

Add the bell pepper, broccoli florets, carrot slices, and snap peas or snow peas to the skillet. Stir-fry for 5-6 minutes until the vegetables are crisp-tender.

Return the tofu to the skillet and pour in the stir-fry sauce. Toss everything together to coat the tofu and vegetables with the sauce. Drizzle with sesame oil, if desired, and sprinkle with sesame seeds for garnish.
Serve the vegan stir-fried tofu and vegetables over cooked rice or noodles.

Nutrition: Calories: 230 | Fat: 12g | Carbohydrates: 18g | Fiber: 4g | Protein: 14g

Cauliflower Buffalo Wings

Prep Time: 15 minutes | **Cook Time:** 25 minutes | **Serve:** 4

Ingredients:
1 head cauliflower, cut into bite-sized florets
1 cup almond flour
1 cup unsweetened plant-based milk (such as almond or soy milk)
1 teaspoon garlic powder
1 teaspoon onion powder
1/2 teaspoon smoked paprika
1/2 teaspoon salt
1/4 teaspoon black pepper
1/2 cup buffalo hot sauce
2 tablespoons vegan butter, melted
Ranch or vegan blue cheese dressing for dipping (optional)
Celery sticks for serving (optional)

Directions:
Preheat the oven to 425°F (220°C). Line a baking sheet with parchment paper.
In a bowl, whisk together the almond flour, plant-based milk, garlic powder, onion powder, smoked paprika, salt, and black pepper to create a batter.
Dip each cauliflower floret into the batter, allowing any excess to drip off, and place it on the prepared baking sheet. Repeat until all the florets are coated.
Bake the cauliflower in the preheated oven for 20 minutes, or until the coating is crispy and golden brown.

In a separate bowl, combine the buffalo hot sauce and melted vegan butter.

Remove the cauliflower from the oven and carefully dip each floret into the buffalo hot sauce mixture, coating it evenly. Place the coated cauliflower back on the baking sheet.

Return the cauliflower to the oven and bake for an additional 5 minutes.

Serve the cauliflower buffalo wings with ranch or vegan blue cheese dressing for dipping and celery sticks on the side, if desired.

Nutrition: Calories: 180 | Fat: 12g | Carbohydrates: 13g | Fiber: 4g | Protein: 7g

Vegan Mushroom Risotto

Prep Time: 10 minutes | **Cook Time:** 40 minutes | **Serve:** 4

Ingredients:
2 tablespoons olive oil
1 onion, finely chopped
3 cloves garlic, minced
8 ounces cremini mushrooms, sliced
1 cup Arborio rice
1/2 cup white wine (optional)
4 cups vegetable broth, warmed
1/2 cup nutritional yeast
1 tablespoon soy sauce or tamari
Salt and pepper to taste
Fresh parsley for garnish (optional)

Directions:
In a large skillet or pan, heat the olive oil over medium heat. Add the chopped onion and minced garlic, and sauté until the onion is translucent.

Add the sliced cremini mushrooms to the pan and cook for 5 minutes, until they release their moisture and start to brown.

Stir in the Arborio rice, coating it with the oil and vegetables. Cook for 1-2 minutes until the rice becomes slightly translucent.

If using, pour in the white wine and stir until it is absorbed by the rice.

Gradually add the warm vegetable broth, about 1/2 cup at a time, stirring constantly and allowing each addition to be absorbed before adding more. Continue this process until the rice is tender and creamy, usually around 25-30 minutes.

Stir in the nutritional yeast and soy sauce or tamari, and season with salt and pepper to taste.

Remove from heat and let the risotto sit for a few minutes to thicken.

Serve the vegan mushroom risotto hot, garnished with fresh parsley if desired.

Nutrition: Calories: 320 | Fat: 8g | Carbohydrates: 52g | Fiber: 5g | Protein: 8g

Protein Recipes

Prep Time: 10 minutes | **Cook Time:** 40 minutes | **Serve:** 6

Ingredients:
1 cup dried green or brown lentils, rinsed and drained
1 tablespoon olive oil
1 onion, diced
3 cloves garlic, minced
2 carrots, diced
2 celery stalks, diced
1 can diced tomatoes (14 oz)
4 cups vegetable broth
2 cups water
1 teaspoon ground cumin
1 teaspoon dried thyme
1 bay leaf
Salt and pepper to taste
Fresh parsley, chopped (for garnish)

Directions:
In a large pot, heat the olive oil over medium heat. Add the diced onion and minced garlic, and sauté until the onion is translucent. Add the diced carrots and celery to the pot, and cook for another 3-4 minutes until slightly tender.
Rinse the lentils under cold water and add them to the pot along with the diced tomatoes, vegetable broth, water, cumin, thyme, bay leaf, salt, and pepper.
Stir well to combine, then bring the soup to a boil.
Reduce the heat to low, cover the pot, and simmer for 30 minutes or until the lentils are cooked and tender.
Remove the bay leaf from the soup.
Using an immersion blender or a countertop blender, blend about half of the soup until smooth. This step is optional and can be adjusted to your preferred consistency.
Taste the soup and adjust the seasonings if needed.

Ladle the Vegan Lentil Soup into bowls and garnish with fresh chopped parsley.
Serve the soup hot and enjoy!

Nutrition: Calories: 200 | Fat: 4g | Carbohydrates: 34g | Fiber: 12g | Protein: 11g

Chickpea Curry

Prep Time: 10 minutes | **Cook Time:** 25 minutes | **Serve:** 4

Ingredients:
1 tablespoon olive oil
1 onion, diced
3 cloves garlic, minced
1 tablespoon curry powder
1 teaspoon ground cumin
1 teaspoon ground coriander
1/2 teaspoon turmeric powder
1/2 teaspoon paprika
1/4 teaspoon cayenne pepper (optional, for heat)
1 can diced tomatoes (14 oz)
1 can coconut milk (14 oz)
2 cans chickpeas, drained and rinsed
1 cup vegetable broth
Salt and pepper to taste
Fresh cilantro, chopped (for garnish)
Cooked rice or naan bread (for serving)

Directions:
In a large skillet, heat the olive oil over medium heat. Add the diced onion and minced garlic, and sauté until the onion is translucent.
Add the curry powder, cumin, coriander, turmeric, paprika, and cayenne pepper (if using) to the skillet. Stir well to coat the onion and garlic with the spices.
Pour in the diced tomatoes (with their juices) and coconut milk. Stir to combine.

Add the drained and rinsed chickpeas to the skillet, along with the vegetable broth. Stir well, then season with salt and pepper to taste.

Bring the mixture to a simmer and let it cook for 15-20 minutes, allowing the flavors to meld together and the sauce to thicken slightly.

Taste the curry and adjust the seasonings if needed.

Serve the Chickpea Curry over cooked rice or with naan bread. Garnish with fresh chopped cilantro.

Enjoy your delicious Chickpea Curry!

Nutrition: Calories: 320 | Fat: 17g | Carbohydrates: 35g | Fiber: 8g | Protein: 9g

Tofu Scramble

Prep Time: 10 minutes | **Cook Time:** 15 minutes | **Serve:** 2

Ingredients:
1 tablespoon olive oil
1/2 onion, diced
1 bell pepper, diced
2 cloves garlic, minced
1 block firm tofu, crumbled
2 tablespoons nutritional yeast
1 teaspoon turmeric
1/2 teaspoon cumin
1/2 teaspoon paprika
Salt and pepper to taste
Fresh parsley or cilantro, chopped (for garnish)
Toast or tortillas (for serving)

Directions:
In a large skillet, heat the olive oil over medium heat. Add the diced onion, bell pepper, and minced garlic. Sauté until the vegetables are softened.

Add the crumbled tofu to the skillet, and cook for 5 minutes, stirring occasionally.

Sprinkle nutritional yeast, turmeric, cumin, paprika, salt, and pepper over the tofu. Stir well to evenly coat the tofu with the spices.

Continue cooking for another 5-7 minutes, until the tofu is heated through and slightly golden.

Taste the tofu scramble and adjust the seasonings if needed.

Remove the skillet from heat and garnish with fresh chopped parsley or cilantro.

Serve the Tofu Scramble with toast or tortillas for a delicious and satisfying breakfast or brunch.

Nutrition: Calories: 180 | Fat: 10g | Carbohydrates: 9g | Fiber: 3g | Protein: 14g

Quinoa Salad with Roasted Vegetables

Prep Time: 15 minutes | **Cook Time:** 25 minutes | **Serve:** 4

Ingredients:
1 cup quinoa, rinsed
2 cups vegetable broth
2 cups mixed vegetables (such as bell peppers, zucchini, eggplant, and cherry tomatoes), diced
2 tablespoons olive oil
1 teaspoon dried oregano
1/2 teaspoon garlic powder
Salt and pepper to taste
1/4 cup fresh parsley, chopped
Juice of 1 lemon
2 tablespoons balsamic vinegar
Optional toppings: avocado slices, toasted nuts or seeds

Directions:
Preheat the oven to 400°F (200°C).

In a saucepan, combine the quinoa and vegetable broth. Bring to a boil, then reduce heat to low, cover, and simmer for 15-20 minutes or until the quinoa is cooked and fluffy. Set aside to cool.

Place the diced mixed vegetables on a baking sheet. Drizzle with olive oil, and sprinkle with dried oregano, garlic powder, salt, and pepper. Toss to coat evenly.

Roast the vegetables in the preheated oven for about 20-25 minutes or until they are tender and slightly caramelized.

In a large bowl, combine the cooked quinoa and roasted vegetables. Add the fresh parsley, lemon juice, and balsamic vinegar. Toss gently to combine.

Taste the salad and adjust the seasonings if needed.

Serve the Quinoa Salad with Roasted Vegetables at room temperature or chilled.

Optional: Top with avocado slices, toasted nuts or seeds for added flavor and texture.

Enjoy this nutritious and flavorful Quinoa Salad as a light and satisfying meal!

Nutrition: Calories: 280 | Fat: 10g | Carbohydrates: 40g | Fiber: 6g | Protein: 8g

Vegan Black Bean Burger

Prep Time: 15 minutes | **Cook Time:** 20 minutes | **Serve:** 4

Ingredients:
1 can (15 ounces) black beans, drained and rinsed
1/2 cup bread crumbs
1/4 cup finely chopped onion
1/4 cup finely chopped bell pepper
2 cloves garlic, minced
2 tablespoons tomato paste
1 tablespoon soy sauce or tamari
1 teaspoon ground cumin
1/2 teaspoon smoked paprika
Salt and pepper to taste
4 burger buns
Optional toppings: lettuce, tomato slices, avocado, vegan mayo

Directions:
In a large bowl, mash the black beans with a fork or potato masher until they are mostly mashed but still have some texture.

Add the bread crumbs, chopped onion, bell pepper, minced garlic, tomato paste, soy sauce, cumin, smoked paprika, salt, and pepper to the bowl. Mix well until all ingredients are combined.

Divide the mixture into 4 equal portions and shape them into patties.
Heat a non-stick skillet over medium heat and lightly grease with oil or cooking spray.
Cook the black bean patties in the skillet for about 4-5 minutes on each side, or until they are golden brown and heated through.
Toast the burger buns if desired.
Assemble the burgers by placing a black bean patty on each bun. Add your preferred toppings such as lettuce, tomato slices, avocado, and vegan mayo.
Serve the Vegan Black Bean Burgers with a side of fries or a fresh salad.

Nutrition: Calories: 250 | Fat: 2g | Carbohydrates: 47g | Fiber: 10g | Protein: 11g

Tempeh Stir-Fry

Prep Time: 15 minutes | **Cook Time:** 15 minutes | **Serve:** 4

Ingredients:
8 ounces tempeh, cubed
2 tablespoons soy sauce or tamari
1 tablespoon rice vinegar
1 tablespoon maple syrup
1 tablespoon sesame oil
1 tablespoon cornstarch
1 tablespoon vegetable oil
1 bell pepper, thinly sliced
1 zucchini, thinly sliced
1 carrot, julienned
2 cloves garlic, minced
1 teaspoon grated ginger
1/4 cup vegetable broth or water
Optional toppings: sliced green onions, sesame seeds

Directions:
In a bowl, combine the soy sauce, rice vinegar, maple syrup, sesame oil, and cornstarch. Stir until the cornstarch is dissolved.

Place the tempeh cubes in the marinade and let them marinate for about 10 minutes.
Heat the vegetable oil in a large skillet or wok over medium heat.
Add the marinated tempeh to the skillet and cook for about 5 minutes, or until the tempeh is browned and crispy.
Remove the tempeh from the skillet and set aside.
In the same skillet, add the bell pepper, zucchini, carrot, garlic, and ginger. Stir-fry for about 5 minutes, or until the vegetables are tender-crisp.
Add the vegetable broth or water to the skillet and stir to deglaze the pan.
Return the cooked tempeh to the skillet and toss to coat it with the vegetables and sauce.
Cook for an additional 1-2 minutes, or until everything is heated through.
Serve the Tempeh Stir-Fry over cooked rice or noodles.
Garnish with sliced green onions and sesame seeds, if desired.

Nutrition: Calories: 220 | Fat: 10g | Carbohydrates: 19g | Fiber: 4g | Protein: 15g

Vegan Chickpea Salad

Prep Time: 10 minutes | **Cook Time:** 0 minutes | **Serve:** 4

Ingredients:
2 cans (15 ounces each) chickpeas, drained and rinsed
1 small red onion, finely chopped
1 bell pepper, diced
1 cucumber, diced
1 cup cherry tomatoes, halved
1/4 cup chopped fresh parsley
2 tablespoons lemon juice
2 tablespoons olive oil
1 teaspoon dijon mustard
Salt and pepper to taste
Optional toppings: avocado slices, sunflower seeds

Directions:
In a large bowl, combine the chickpeas, red onion, bell pepper, cucumber, cherry tomatoes, and fresh parsley.
In a small bowl, whisk together the lemon juice, olive oil, dijon mustard, salt, and pepper.
Pour the dressing over the chickpea mixture and toss to combine all the ingredients.
Adjust the seasoning according to your taste preferences.
Let the salad sit for about 10 minutes to allow the flavors to meld together.
Serve the Vegan Chickpea Salad as is or over a bed of mixed greens.
Garnish with avocado slices and sunflower seeds, if desired.

Nutrition: Calories: 230 | Fat: 8g | Carbohydrates: 32g | Fiber: 9g | Protein: 10g

Dessert

Vegan Chocolate Chip Cookies

Prep Time: 15 minutes | **Cook Time:** 12 minutes | **Serve:** 12 cookies

Ingredients:
1 1/4 cups all-purpose flour
1/2 teaspoon baking soda
1/2 teaspoon salt
1/2 cup coconut oil, melted
1/2 cup brown sugar
1/4 cup granulated sugar
1/4 cup unsweetened applesauce
1 teaspoon vanilla extract
1 cup vegan chocolate chips

Directions:
Preheat the oven to 350°F (175°C) and line a baking sheet with parchment paper.
In a medium bowl, whisk together the flour, baking soda, and salt.
In a large bowl, cream together the melted coconut oil, brown sugar, and granulated sugar until well combined.
Add the applesauce and vanilla extract to the wet ingredients and mix until smooth.
Gradually add the dry ingredients to the wet ingredients, stirring until just combined.
Fold in the vegan chocolate chips.
Scoop tablespoon-sized portions of dough onto the prepared baking sheet, spacing them apart to allow for spreading.
Bake for 10-12 minutes or until the edges are golden brown.
Remove from the oven and let the cookies cool on the baking sheet for 5 minutes, then transfer them to a wire rack to cool completely.

Nutrition: Calories: 180 | Fat: 9g | Carbohydrates: 25g | Fiber: 1g | Protein: 2g

Prep Time: 15 minutes | **Cook Time:** 1 hour | **Serve:** 10 slices

Ingredients:
3 ripe bananas, mashed
1/2 cup coconut oil, melted
1/2 cup maple syrup or agave nectar
1 teaspoon vanilla extract
1 3/4 cups all-purpose flour
1 teaspoon baking soda
1/2 teaspoon salt
1/2 teaspoon ground cinnamon
1/4 teaspoon ground nutmeg
1/2 cup chopped walnuts or pecans (optional)

Directions:
Preheat the oven to 350°F (175°C) and lightly grease a 9x5-inch loaf pan.
In a large mixing bowl, combine the mashed bananas, melted coconut oil, maple syrup or agave nectar, and vanilla extract. Mix well.
In a separate bowl, whisk together the flour, baking soda, salt, cinnamon, and nutmeg.
Gradually add the dry ingredients to the wet ingredients, stirring until just combined. Be careful not to overmix.
If using, fold in the chopped walnuts or pecans.
Pour the batter into the prepared loaf pan and spread it evenly.
Bake for 55-60 minutes or until a toothpick inserted into the center comes out clean.
Remove from the oven and let the banana bread cool in the pan for 10 minutes, then transfer it to a wire rack to cool completely before slicing.

Nutrition: Calories: 240 | Fat: 12g | Carbohydrates: 32g | Fiber: 2g | Protein: 3g

Prep Time: 15 minutes | **Cook Time:** 30 minutes | **Serve:** 12

Ingredients:
1 1/2 cups all-purpose flour
1 cup granulated sugar
1/3 cup unsweetened cocoa powder
1 teaspoon baking soda
1/2 teaspoon salt
1 cup brewed coffee, cooled
1/2 cup unsweetened applesauce
1/3 cup vegetable oil
2 teaspoons vanilla extract
1 tablespoon apple cider vinegar
Vegan frosting of your choice

Directions:
Preheat the oven to 350°F (175°C) and lightly grease a 9-inch round cake pan.
In a large mixing bowl, whisk together the flour, sugar, cocoa powder, baking soda, and salt.
In a separate bowl, combine the brewed coffee, applesauce, vegetable oil, and vanilla extract.
Pour the wet ingredients into the dry ingredients and stir until just combined. Be careful not to overmix.
Add the apple cider vinegar to the batter and stir until evenly distributed.
Pour the batter into the prepared cake pan and smooth the top with a spatula.
Bake for approximately 30 minutes or until a toothpick inserted into the center comes out clean.
Remove the cake from the oven and let it cool in the pan for 10 minutes, then transfer it to a wire rack to cool completely.
Once the cake has cooled, frost it with your favorite vegan frosting. You can choose a classic chocolate frosting, vegan cream cheese frosting, or any other flavor you prefer.
Slice and serve the delicious Vegan Chocolate Cake to enjoy its rich and moist texture.

Vegan Peanut Butter Cups

Prep Time: 15 minutes | **Cook Time:** 0 minutes | **Serve:** 12

Ingredients:
1 cup vegan chocolate chips
1/2 cup creamy peanut butter
2 tablespoons maple syrup
1/4 teaspoon vanilla extract
Pinch of salt

Directions:
Line a muffin tin with 12 paper or silicone liners.
In a microwave-safe bowl, melt the vegan chocolate chips in 30-second intervals, stirring in between, until smooth and melted.
Spoon approximately 1 tablespoon of melted chocolate into the bottom of each liner, spreading it to form a thin layer.
Place the muffin tin in the refrigerator to allow the chocolate to set, about 10 minutes.
In a separate bowl, mix together the peanut butter, maple syrup, vanilla extract, and salt until well combined.
Remove the muffin tin from the refrigerator and spoon approximately 1 tablespoon of the peanut butter mixture on top of each chocolate layer.
Gently spread the peanut butter mixture to cover the chocolate, leaving a small border around the edges.
Return the muffin tin to the refrigerator to set for another 10 minutes.
Once the peanut butter has firmed up, remove the muffin tin from the refrigerator and spoon the remaining melted chocolate over the peanut butter layer, covering it completely.
Place the muffin tin back in the refrigerator and let it set for at least 1 hour, or until the chocolate is firm.
Once fully set, remove the peanut butter cups from the muffin tin and store them in an airtight container in the refrigerator.

Nutrition: Calories: 150 | Fat: 9g | Carbohydrates: 15g | Fiber: 2g | Protein: 3g

Vegan Blueberry Muffins

Prep Time: 15 minutes | **Cook Time:** 25 minutes | **Serve:** 12

Ingredients:
2 cups all-purpose flour
1/2 cup granulated sugar
1 tablespoon baking powder
1/2 teaspoon salt
1 cup non-dairy milk (such as almond or soy milk)
1/4 cup melted coconut oil or vegetable oil
1 teaspoon vanilla extract
1 cup fresh or frozen blueberries

Directions:
Preheat the oven to 375°F (190°C) and line a muffin tin with 12 paper or silicone liners.
In a large mixing bowl, whisk together the flour, sugar, baking powder, and salt.
In a separate bowl, mix together the non-dairy milk, melted coconut oil or vegetable oil, and vanilla extract.
Pour the wet ingredients into the dry ingredients and stir until just combined. Be careful not to overmix; a few lumps are okay.
Gently fold in the blueberries, being careful not to crush them.
Divide the batter evenly among the prepared muffin cups, filling each about three-quarters full.
Bake in the preheated oven for 20 to 25 minutes, or until a toothpick inserted into the center of a muffin comes out clean.
Remove the muffins from the oven and let them cool in the tin for 5 minutes, then transfer them to a wire rack to cool completely.

Nutrition: Calories: 180 | Fat: 6g | Carbohydrates: 29g | Fiber: 1g | Protein: 3g

Prep Time: 30 minutes | **Cook Time:** 45 minutes | **Serve:** 8

Ingredients:
For the crust:
1 1/2 cups vegan graham cracker crumbs
1/4 cup melted coconut oil
2 tablespoons maple syrup
For the filling:
2 cups raw cashews (soaked in water for at least 4 hours or overnight, then drained)
1/2 cup coconut cream
1/2 cup maple syrup
1/4 cup lemon juice
1 teaspoon vanilla extract
For the raspberry sauce:
1 cup fresh or frozen raspberries
2 tablespoons maple syrup
1 tablespoon lemon juice

Directions:
In a bowl, combine the graham cracker crumbs, melted coconut oil, and maple syrup for the crust. Stir until the mixture resembles wet sand.
Press the crust mixture into the bottom of a 9-inch springform pan to create an even layer. Place it in the freezer to set while you prepare the filling.
In a blender or food processor, combine the soaked cashews, coconut cream, maple syrup, lemon juice, and vanilla extract. Blend until smooth and creamy.
Pour the filling over the prepared crust in the springform pan. Smooth the top with a spatula.
In a small saucepan, combine the raspberries, maple syrup, and lemon juice for the raspberry sauce. Cook over medium heat until the raspberries break down and the mixture thickens slightly, about 5 minutes. Remove from heat and let it cool.
Drizzle the raspberry sauce over the top of the cheesecake filling, then use a toothpick or a knife to create a swirl pattern.

Place the cheesecake in the refrigerator and let it chill for at least 4 hours or overnight until firm.

Before serving, remove the cheesecake from the springform pan and slice into individual servings.

Nutrition: Calories: 340 | Fat: 23g | Carbohydrates: 30g | Fiber: 2g | Protein: 6g

---

Vegan Coconut Bliss Balls

Prep Time: 15 minutes | **Cook Time:** / | **Serve:** 12 balls

Ingredients:
1 cup dates, pitted
1 cup unsweetened shredded coconut
1/4 cup almond butter
2 tablespoons maple syrup
1 tablespoon coconut oil
1 teaspoon vanilla extract
Pinch of salt

Directions:
In a food processor, combine the pitted dates, shredded coconut, almond butter, maple syrup, coconut oil, vanilla extract, and a pinch of salt. Process until the mixture comes together and forms a sticky dough.

Scoop about a tablespoon of the dough and roll it between your hands to form a ball. Repeat with the remaining dough.

Optional: Roll the balls in additional shredded coconut for extra coconut flavor and texture.

Place the coconut bliss balls on a baking sheet lined with parchment paper and refrigerate for at least 30 minutes to firm up.

Once chilled, the coconut bliss balls are ready to serve. Enjoy them as a healthy snack or dessert.

Nutrition: Calories: 120 | Fat: 6g | Carbohydrates: 16g | Fiber: 2g | Protein: 1g

Conclusion

In conclusion, this book has provided a comprehensive exploration of veganism, covering everything from understanding the ethical foundations to mastering essential kitchen skills and embracing a vegan lifestyle. Throughout its chapters, you have gained valuable knowledge about the principles and values that underpin veganism, the health benefits of a plant-based diet, and practical tips for meal planning, cooking, and entertaining.

You have discovered that veganism is not just about personal well-being but also about compassion and respect for all sentient beings. By choosing a vegan lifestyle, you are making a positive impact on the environment, reducing the risk of chronic diseases, and promoting overall well-being. You have learned about the importance of balanced nutrition, the essential pantry items for vegan cooking, and the techniques to master in the kitchen.

Moreover, this book has highlighted the significance of veganism in various aspects of life, including family and children, fitness and sports performance, beauty and personal care, and even activism. You have been inspired to raise vegan children, explore vegan-friendly beauty products, and become an advocate for animals and the planet.

As you conclude your journey through the pages of this book, remember that veganism is not just a diet or a trend—it is a compassionate and conscious way of living. It is a commitment to making choices that align with your values, and it is a powerful tool for positive change.

Now armed with knowledge, skills, and motivation, you are ready to embark on your own vegan journey. Embrace the joy of discovering new flavors, the satisfaction of nourishing your body with wholesome plant-based foods, and the fulfillment of making a difference in the world. Remember, every meal, every choice, and every action matters.

As you close this book, I encourage you to carry the spirit of veganism in your heart and share it with others. Spread the word, lead by example, and inspire those around you to embrace a vegan lifestyle. Together, we can create a kinder, more compassionate world for humans, animals, and the planet we all call home.

Thank you for joining us on this transformative journey. May your vegan path be filled with health, happiness, and boundless compassion.